~ *Hamburg Cove* ~

The Lyme Historical Society gratefully acknowledges contributions
for the publication of this book from:

Cynthia & Louis Bacon
Rufus Barringer
Dr. & Mrs. Arnold Baskin
Mr. & Mrs. Rudolph F. Besier
Sally J. Bill
Mr. & Mrs. Howard D. Brundage
Harold & Ann Buttrick
Mr. & Mrs. Valentine B. Chamberlain, III
Mr. & Mrs. Jeffrey F. Clark
Adele Clement
Richard F. Cooper, Jr.
Mr. & Mrs. Robert H. Cushman
Dorothy Czikowsky
Paul K. Darcy
William & Patricia DeMatteo
Dunham Ltd., Realtors
Mr. & Mrs. Jeb N. Embree
Barbara P. Ferry
Lytt & Sis Gould
Mr. & Mrs. Michael W. Gourlay
Paul & Eleanor Harper
Roger & Eleanor Hilsman
Mr. & Mrs. Albert C. Hine
Nancy Hine & Joel Schwartz
Mr. & Mrs. H. Everton Hosley, Jr.
Margaret B. & Arthur Howe, Jr.
Josephine P. Irvine in memory of husband Jan Irvine and artist William Irvine
Dr. & Mrs. William D. Irving
Jonathan Isleib
Mr. & Mrs. Charles S. Jewett
Mr. & Mrs. Charles W. Jewett
Edwina W. P. Johnson
Mrs. Adolph Kastelowitz
Carol Hardin Kimball
Dr. & Mrs Robert J. Klimek
Mr. & Mrs. Roland S. MacNichol
Gretchen & Mowry Mann
In loving memory of Hiram Hamilton Maxim by Marti & Hiram P. Maxim
Drs. Margaret & Earl Mummert
Robert M. & Mary Beth Petitt
Mr. & Mrs. Ernest D. Pierog
Gary H. Reynolds
Joe & Virginia Rhodes
Ben Rosenthal & Nelle Davis
Cynthia Rowley
Paul & Eva Schimert
Mr. & Mrs. Michael H. Sherwood
Joan & Lee Sillin
Mr. & Mrs. Bernard M. Slater
Mr. & Mrs. Harold C. Todd, Jr.
Dr. & Mrs. William H. Umberger
Mr. & Mrs. George J. Willauer
Mr. & Mrs. Thomas Wing
Mr. & Mrs. Charles T. Young, III

and others whose gifts arrived after the manuscript
had been sent to the publisher.

The Lymes' Heritage Series

HAMBURG ~ COVE ~

STANLEY SCHULER, *editor*

LYME HISTORICAL SOCIETY
FLORENCE GRISWOLD MUSEUM
Old Lyme, Connecticut

FRONT COVER: Reed's Landing, *1840, as seen by G.F. Bottum (1828-1879).*
The artist is looking north up the Eight Mile River toward Old Hamburg Bridge.
Old Hamburg Road is on the right; Joshuatown Road on the left. Oil on canvas.
OWNED BY THE TOWN OF LYME AND HANGING IN THE LYME TOWN HALL. PHOTO BY SKIP HINE.

BACK COVER: *The Lower Bay, Hamburg Cove, as seen by Hugh de Haven. See*
the companion painting on page 23.

~

~ CONTENTS ~

Czikowsky's Hill *by Richard L. Brooks. The view from Joshuatown Road, high on Czikowsky's Hill, across Hamburg Cove's Upper Bay toward Hamburg and the hills beyond is one of the most frequently painted and photographed scenes in the lower Connecticut River Valley. Oil on canvas.* COLLECTION OF CAPT. AND MRS. ROBERT GUSTAFSON. PHOTO BY SKIP HINE.

~ *Hamburg Cove* ~

∼ I ∼

INTIMATE, BEAUTIFUL HAMBURG COVE

by STANLEY SCHULER

What is there about Hamburg Cove that has persuaded artists to paint it so often—more often than any other single feature or area of the whole lower Connecticut River Valley? The painters themselves cannot answer—not in words, that is. People in the arts are generally articulate only in their personal specialty. Trying to speak for them, I think the answer to the question lies in the intimacy, immediacy, and quiet of the Cove. And, of course, in its very special beauty.

Contrary to what you may think, the answer is not in the Cove's beauty alone. Many areas of the Connecticut River Valley are equally beautiful. Years ago, soon after my wife and I moved to Lyme, we bought a canoe and in a moment of complete idiocy took it out on the big river on the Fourth of July. It was a marvelous day and as we paddled north from the town landing at the end of Ely's Ferry Road, we exclaimed at the beauty of the outcropping rocks and trees overhanging the water. But not for long. It was rather late in the afternoon and suddenly we were bobbing and rocking in the wakes of the powerboats roaring home to Hartford, Branford, and Long Island. I had paddled across Grand Lake Matagamon in Maine in heavy wind and down the East Branch of the Penobscot (overturning once) with total lack of concern. But the Connecticut River was frightening, and we never went canoeing on it again.

By contrast, Hamburg Cove—an arm of the Connecticut—is always serene. Yes, there are times when the residents along the shore would happily throttle noisy boaters. But even at its noisiest, the Cove is peace. Just the other day I stood on the bank at the juncture of Abigail's Hole and the Lower Bay and watched two specks moving into the Cove. The sun was high in the cloudless sky, but it was a cool autumn day with a breeze riffling the water and occasionally puffing clouds of red and yellow leaves out over it. Slowly the two specks came closer —first, a man in a kayak, the blades of his double paddle alternately dipping into the water and circling, glistening, in the air; then, about fifty yards behind, a canoe with two occupants, the woman in the bow with a reddish umbrella opened and extended before her to catch the breeze like a sail. The two craft passed, silhouetted against the sunrays bouncing off the water, almost lost momentarily in the glare, then emerging, happy, unconcerned, at peace.

You might, on the rare day when motorized traffic is sparse, see the same thing on the Connecticut. But it would not really be the same, because even in the tightest valleys the river is big, reaching out to a wide world, whereas the Cove is small, like a parent's arms spread to encircle a home-coming child. It is, as I said, intimate. Immediate in its closeness. And in the absence of dissenting voices, I suspect this is what attracts painters and everyone else to it.

And for the most part, the painters' oils and watercolors and pastels reflect this.

We might wish, however, that they were sometimes on hand to record the truly breathtaking, soul-moving scenes the Cove is wont to insert between acts:

The May afternoon when you're standing on a terrace high above the Lower Bay that is seemingly spread directly below. You feel like the soaring eagle searching for fish, but now the water is specked with boats that from the distance seem no larger than fish. The land is green—the soft awakening green of oaks and maples accented by the black green of conifers. The sky is blue but partially hidden by huge racing, roiling clouds threatening a storm. The sun, nearing the hills of Essex, breaks through for a half minute and the water glares; then the sun disappears and the water is gray. In another minute the sun reappears, lighting a different part of the landscape; then goes. The sequence repeats again and again, and each time, because the sun is sinking rapidly and because of the shapes of the clouds crossing below it, the picture changes.

The December afternoon when the setting sun erupts from the black, low-hanging clouds that have obscured it all day and the hills and trees and rocks and houses—everything except the surly-looking water—turn pinkish orange-red.

The January day when you're lunching at a home above the narrowest part of the Narrows. It is high noon on a brilliant day, but the sun barely penetrates the hemlocks thronging the steep banks on either side of the water twenty or so feet below you. The water is like black ink, without perceptible motion except for a little pan of ice that inches by.

If I were a painter, I know why I would paint Hamburg Cove.

The real painters let their paintings speak for themselves.

∾

STANLEY SCHULER *has written many, many books and magazine and newspaper articles. He has also edited magazines and books. He lived in Lyme for eighteen years before moving to Old Lyme.*

∼ II ∼

A BLESSED PLACE

by CAPTAIN ROBERT B. GUSTAFSON
with JOSEPH GRIBBINS

This blessed place is roughly halfway between Boston and New York, about seven and one-half miles above the lighthouse at Saybrook breakwater where the Connecticut River meets Long Island Sound, about a mile above Essex, and just opposite Brockway Island on the east bank of the river that goes north to Hartford and south to the world. Bounded by high, wooded hills and much like a fjord, deep almost to its steep green banks, it is renowned as one of the most protected and charming anchorages in Connecticut. For decades boating people have sought its shelter as a "hurricane hole" in threatening weather and, on summer days of big blue skies and sunshine, as a place to swim, fish, anchor for the night, or for a weekend or an hour just to absorb its peace and green scenery.

As early as 1817, the Boston *Transcript* described this place as "…an earthly paradise. Broadening a bit as you ascend it, the waters are covered with a luxuriant mass of wild rice. Cardinal flowers grow along the margin of the water in a passionate splendor of color."[1] In 1972 *A Cruising Guide to the New England Coast*

Hamburg Cove from its entrance on the east side of the Connecticut River. The Lower Bay extends to the Narrows (upper left); beyond the Narrows, the Upper Bay (extreme upper left) opens out. The latter is much larger than it appears here. Abigail's Hole is at center left, below the tree-edged open fields. PHOTO BY AERO SERVICE DIVISION, LITTON INDUSTRIES.

called it a "delightful and beautiful spot."[2] In 1972 and again in 1992 *The Waterway Guide* praised its "total protection and magnificent natural surroundings."[3] An article in the August 29, 1992 edition of the *Pictorial Gazette* found it "an unparalleled anchorage...Its bordering rocks, forests and cliffs are breathtakingly beautiful."[4]

This blessed place is Hamburg Cove, Lyme, Connecticut, and all the above descriptions are accurate. Nothing essential has changed since 1817 or, for all we know, since Adriaen Block sailed up the Connecticut River in 1614 or since the dugout canoes of the Indians passed over these waters. The Cove is actually a portion of the Eight Mile River, which flows southward eight miles to the Connecticut River from Devil's Hopyard and Salem. Hamburg Cove consists of two "bays" and their channels. These comprise the navigable portion of the Eight Mile River between the Connecticut River and the village of Hamburg. At various time the bays have been called the Upper Bay, the Inner Cove, the Upper Cove, the Hamburg Basin, and the Lower Bay, the Great Bay, the Lower Cove, and the Outer Cove. Old-timers seem to prefer the terms "Upper Bay" and "Lower Bay." The design of the Hamburg Cove Yacht Club's burgee may best define the geographical configuration of the Cove—a "lazy eight" representing the two bays and the Eight Mile River.

Throughout the seasons the Cove offers sharp contrasts—from the variety, activity, and sound of a hundred yachts crowded together on a hot summer weekend to the stark stillness of a winter's day with a lone bald eagle circling majestically over ice and snow.

Spring

By the start of spring, most of the ice has left the Cove, the water is crystal clear, and the sandy bottom is visible along the shoreline. Here and there is scattered debris left from winter storms and high tides—derelict rowboats, errant mooring buoys cut adrift by the ice, tree trunks and branches that have traveled down the Con-

Modern Old Hamburg (Joshuatown) Bridge crosses the extreme northern end of Hamburg Cove, or what is actually known at this point as the Eight Mile River.

necticut River from faraway places. A lot of this debris is flushed out by the high spring tides and freshets, and continues its journey down the river to the Sound.

Bald eagles may still be around in early spring, but the first human intrusions usually chase them away. These are the fishermen in small outboards, out early in the cold, damp, and often rainy mornings, impatient to catch the first white perch. Then the first yacht appears, usually with a new owner eager to test his new toy. Although the eagles disappear, their relatives—the hawks and osprey—remain. The seagulls never leave. Then the Cove's one and only pair of swans appears, in straight-line formation with their new cygnets between them.

In the Upper Bay a flurry of activity begins at the marinas.

Boats are uncovered, cleaned, sanded, and painted, and the ritual of fitting-out continues until summer. In April a crew from Cove Landing starts "planting" the moorings. Each fresh-painted buoy with chain, swivels, shackles, and mushroom anchor is carefully lowered into the water of the Lower Bay in rows to suit the harbormaster's grid plan. Before the job is completed, a few early-bird boats will have picked up their moorings for the new season. After the moorings have been placed, the same crew sets the channel markers and buoys. (Until the Town of Lyme recently funded the cost of this work, it had been done since the early 1940s by Charles S. Jewett.) Gradually the boats come to their moorings clean and freshly painted and varnished. Except for the schooner *Golden Goose*, which is always shipshape and Bristol fashion, the wooden and older boats are always the last to arrive.

By the middle of May, the trees have sprung to life and the hills and shores are colored a delicate green. About the middle of June, the mountain laurel, abundant along the shoreline, blossoms in all its glory. Pink lady's slippers spring from decaying logs and needle-carpeted soil.

Summer

Summer begins as the laurel blossoms fade and fall. Boats of all types and sizes begin to visit the Cove—rowing shells, canoes, inflatables, outboards, power cruisers, sailboats, houseboats, tour boats, workboats, and one or two antique steam launches. Tugboats with barges or pile drivers come in to repair docks and seawalls damaged by the winter ice. The stately schooner *Brilliant* comes in to spend the night after completing her fitting-out at the Essex Boat Works and before sailing home to Mystic Seaport.

On the first warm weekend, as many as a hundred boats will moor in the Lower Bay. Suddenly the Cove is a vibrant scene. But on Monday morning only a dozen or so boats will remain, the rest having returned to their home moorings and marinas.

On a typical weekday, dawn breaks with a windless morning

Below Hamburg Bridge, the rushing, rocky Eight Mile River widens out and flows quietly into Hamburg Cove's Upper Bay (not visible here). The river is bordered on both sides by houses, many of them ancient.

and the Cove is perfectly still with mirror images of boats reflecting on its surface. Several deer—part of the large herd that regularly feeds in one of the fields on Ely's Ferry Road—are drinking on the wooded shore. Sometimes a red fox is nearby. A wild turkey hen with five or six poults ranging around her marches through the woods foraging for food but ever alert for trouble. The spell is broken by the sound of a three-horsepower outboard motor on a small dinghy or inflatable as its child skipper, bored after breakfast and full of sugared cereal, circles around the sleeping boats waiting for the action to begin. The Cove gradually comes to life as a few boats leave their moorings, break the silky surface of the water, and gently rock the sleeping boats with their wakes. The sleepers stir and poke their heads out of hatches, then come on deck with cups of coffee in hand. A few dive over the side for a refreshing swim before breakfast. Shortly after nine the day's breeze stirs, and a few more boats sail out of the channel to the river. Throughout the day some depart, some remain, and new boats come in.

For the lucky people aboard the boats that stay or arrive, this will be a lazy day of swimming, sunbathing, dinghy sailing, fishing, exploring the Cove, getting ice and supplies at the village, then rafting up with other boats for cocktail hour and a steak dinner cooked on rail-mounted charcoal grills. Shortly before sunset the lovely 70-foot schooner *Phoenix* from Essex, which offers trips for individuals and private parties, glides into the Cove with all sails set. *Phoenix* maneuvers through the fleet, then silently turns and sails into the sunset just as in the movies.

After watching a spectacular sunset, the boatmen lower their flags and go below. One by one, cabin and anchor lights are turned on, and soon in the darkness an array of lights reflect and dance on the water. This day's routine repeats itself throughout the summer but with different boats and different people. The boats that visit the Cove come down from Maine and up from Florida, and from every place in between. The *Gjoa*, now homeported in Lyme, came all the way from San Francisco. Most boats now proudly display their true home ports, but a few still practice the "Delaware Dodge" and display "Wilmington" or "Dover" on their transoms even though the waters of the First State have never wet their hulls. There are tax advantages in being a Delaware-registered boat.

Some classic wooden boats visit Hamburg Cove year after year. One of them is *Flora*, a former working oyster boat, now owned by Essex Boat Works and beautifully restored in their shops. *Flora* often visits the Lower Cove in the summer with a piano on deck and with an accompaniment of banjos, trumpet, and tuba to give an evening concert of old favorites. The fleet sounds bells and horns after each number in spontaneous appreciation. *Flora* is also a favorite in the annual Mystic Seaport Antique and Classic Boat Parade. Then there is *Duchess*, homeported at Cove Landing, which usually leads the Mystic parade. In 1992 Mystic's "Best in Show" award was given to *Nor' Easter*, a 65-year-old 60-foot motorsailer that normally winters at Cove Landing. Other classics in the Cove are *Golden Goose*, *Panda*, *Happy*, *Blueberry*, *Snowbird*, *Valentine*, *Lauralee*, *Gjoa*, *Blackjack*, and the two steam launches *Osprey* and *Loon*.

Along the southeast shore of the channel, just before the narrows that lead into the Upper Bay, is a summer camp for children. It is high above the water and not visible from the Cove except for a small boathouse on the shore. This is Camp Claire, serving children grades 3 through 9, and established at Hamburg Cove in 1916 by the First Congregational Church in Meriden. Camp Claire has been in operation every summer since its founding and is generally open for the months of July and August. The camp has about eighty boy and girl campers and a staff of twenty. Its fleet of canoes can frequently be seen with youngsters paddling in formation to and from the Connecticut River. Camp Claire never changes—grace sung before meals, evening vespers, swimming and canoes, sunshine and the sheer beauty of this special place.

For the past twenty-six years, Hamburg Cove has had an unorganized, do-it-yourself Fourth of July parade on Cove Road that has grown to a mile-long gathering of floats, fire engines, antique cars, horses, tractors, and marchers in homemade costumes. It culminates in a "Lyme Tea Party" at the bridge where Falls Brook enters the Upper Bay. The parade's founder, Dr. William Irving, says a few words about the Declaration of Independence and the colonists who fought for our freedom. Then the teabags go into the Cove and the cannons are fired. (Lyme really did have an imitation of the Boston Tea Party when, on March 17, 1774, a peddler came to town with about a hundred pounds of tea imported after the Tea Act. The Lyme patriots promptly confiscated the tea and burned it.)[5] For visitors to the Cove, it is an event not to be missed.

Another annual event of interest to the Cove's summer visi-

The northern end of the Upper Bay early in the 1900s. The hill is locally known as Czikowsky's Hill. The area high above the house is Candlewood Ledge, so called because the pitch pines growing there were once split into slivers used as candles. COLLECTION OF ELIZEBETH B. PLIMPTON.

tors is the Hamburg Fair, held on a weekend about the middle of August. The day after Labor Day, the Essex Rotary Club holds its annual steak cookout aboard *Flora* and the barge *Walrus* in the Lower Bay. The sound of Stu Ingersoll's banjo and brass band not only entertains the fleet, but the aroma of charcoal-grilled steaks whets every appetite.

After Labor Day, the number of boats in the Lower Bay begins to decline, even though September is probably the best month to visit this magical place. The days are clear and warm and the nights refreshingly cool. The water is still warm enough for swimming. Near the end of September, the greenery begins to display fall's brilliant colors, and soon hills and shoreline are a blaze of reds, golds, faded greens, and yellows. Summer on the Cove is over.

Autumn

Season's end for the boats in Hamburg Cove is usually the Columbus Day weekend, often the peak of the foliage season. The Ram Island Yacht Club, the Baldwin Bridge Yacht Club (a unique club without a formal organization or clubhouse—just boats), and others come to the Cove for a giant rendezvous. They raft up together in sizable groups—twenty or more—and boats stretch across the Lower Bay. Sometimes this gets interesting when the tide changes! They hold a variety of dinghy races, parties, and raftups, and seem to have a barrel of fun. Sometimes they get a bonus with a beautiful harvest moon during their stay.

In the Upper Bay the marinas are busy hauling, covering, and storing boats for the winter. The weather grows colder and leaves are soon gone from the trees.

Cove Landing or Old Lyme Marina crews begin to pull the moorings—a wet, dirty, laborious task. Then the channel markers are removed. By Thanksgiving most of the boats are gone. A few years ago the Cove froze over at Thanksgiving time and a big, beautiful racing yacht was frozen in and suffered damage when it was stuck all winter.

But the Cove does not normally freeze completely over until the middle of December. When it does, the surface is smooth and like a huge mirror. Then the rise and fall of the tide causes cracks to form and there are loud zinging noises as the cracks race across the surface. This is an especially eerie performance at night. After the first snow covers the ice like a soft blanket, and the tree branches, especially the hemlocks, are heavily laden, the whole Cove becomes, literally, a winter wonderland—just in time for a white Christmas.

Winter

Despite its beauty, winter ice can be very damaging. Responding to the tide, it can pull out pilings and break up docks and floats. It can pull 40-foot steel I-beam pilings completely out of the bottom or bend pipe pilings like pretzels. Permanent docks have a poor survival record in the Cove. Floating docks that can be hauled by the marinas or pulled out on the shore for the winter are better to use.

In the early 1920s ice was still harvested on the Cove for both commercial and private use. It was stored in icehouses with thick double walls filled with sawdust for insulation. The Knickerbocker Ice Company had an icehouse at a point on the eastern shore of the Lower Bay called Flat Rock, where ice was hauled, stored, and shipped to New York by coasting schooners. In the 1700s Flat Rock was a landing where heavy goods could be offloaded from vessels and transported by oxcart along a road to the mills on Falls Brook. Remnants of a large timber bulkhead can still be seen at Flat Rock. Residents also cut and stored ice at various locations on the Cove for their own use throughout the summer.

These days, fishermen venture out on the ice whenever it seems thick enough to cut holes for fishing or spearing eels. The Upper Bay is a popular spot to ice-fish—and a safe one because of the shallow water. And you can skate on the Cove in the depths of winter. It's fun to skate from the Lower Bay to the Upper Bay, but be prepared to go against the wind on the return trip. Back in the winter of 1935-36, Leland Reynolds of Reynolds Garage and Marina drove a car on the ice from Hamburg to Essex and back. He said it was a car that had been recently damaged, and he felt it would not be much of a loss if it fell through the ice, so he gave it a try and made it.

Leland had another dangerous adventure on the Cove some years later. In the early 1970s there was a motel and marina at Saybrook that some residents thought was owned by "the Mob." Whoever these "Mobsters" were, they also owned a few good-looking 40- to 50-foot powerboats that frequented the Lower Bay. Leland Reynolds liked to pull his marina's moorings early, before the cold weather set in. One day he pulled all his moorings but the one to which a "Mob" boat was tied. Leland brought his workboat alongside and told the man on deck what he was about to do. He asked that they leave and pick up another mooring. In short order an argument developed, and standing on shore I heard the commotion and watched as the deckhand ran below to get the owner. Suddenly a burly gentleman came out of the cabin with a pistol in hand. He fired two shots into the air and then pointed the gun at Leland and shouted that the next shots were for him. Leland left without his mooring.

Perhaps the best part of the winter season is when the ice begins to break up, and there is some open water in the Lower Bay and no human activity on the Cove. This is when the bald eagles catch fish. They soar in circles over the Cove until their sharp eyes spot a fish. Then they plummet down and grab the fish with their extended talons without their bodies touching the water (unlike the ospreys that plunge right in). If it is a small fish, the eagle flies to a tree like a torpedo bomber with its weapon in launching position. If it is a large fish, the eagle likes to land on the nearest ice to start the feast. Within a few seconds, crows and sea-gulls arrive and form two circles surrounding the eagle—crows on the inside and gulls on the outside. The size of the circles gradually shrinks as crows and gulls creep ever closer. Suddenly the eagle raises his head and spreads his wings, and the scavengers back off to start the performance all over again. After a satisfying meal, the eagle will fly off and sometimes leave the remains for the crows and seagulls to squabble over. The crows are bolder and more aggressive than the gulls.

When two or more eagles are fishing at the same time, they seem never to compete with one another. A special treat is to watch the eagles teach their young to fish by playing "follow the leader." The adult eagle glides over the water searching for fish as the young bird follows closely behind. When the adult swoops down to pick up a fish, the young eagle makes the same move and learns quickly. The young perches beside the parent in trees along the Cove to share the catch and to watch for more fish near the surface.

As soon as human activity on the Cove begins—perhaps just a few outboard motors passing through—the eagles are suddenly gone and the winter season is over. (This was not always so. In 1952, a mating pair of eagles nested along Hamburg Cove year-round and produced a baby there.[6] Scientists believe the great birds did this more or less regularly before that time. What drove them away—as it drove away the ospreys—was DDT, which got into the food chain and caused female eagles to lay fragile eggs that broke.)

~

Hamburg Cove is, of course, a public place. Unfortunately, it cannot be enjoyed to the fullest by all members of the public. Those on foot, bicycle, or horseback or in automobiles are limited in what they can see. For them, the best views—of the Upper Bay only—are from the Cove Road bridge across the mouth of Falls Brook and from about halfway up Czikowsky's Hill on Joshua-town Road. A much more restricted view of the Upper Bay is from Joshuatown bridge and the two roads leading to it. The Lower Bay can be seen—but only through trees—from the northern half of Cove Road.

Homeowners on the banks of the Cove and hills around it fare better, but in no case can they see all parts of the Cove from their houses.

For maximum enjoyment of the entire Cove, you must come by boat—as hundreds of people do. Here is how you will see it:

A pair of buoys maintained by the U.S. Coast Guard (Green Can #1 and Red Nun #2) mark the narrow entrance channel that leads into the Lower Bay and the principal anchorage area. The channel has a charted depth of 9 feet and is marked by town-maintained buoys and stake markers. But the marked channel must be slowly and carefully followed, or the errant skipper will find his vessel high and dry in as little as a foot of water at low tide. The wooded shoreline on both sides of the entrance is under the guardianship of the Nature Conservancy, the Connecticut River Gateway Conservation Zone, the Lyme Conservation and Wetlands Commission, and certain scenic easements donated to the State of Connecticut.

There is a shallow cove called Abigail's Hole north of Green Can Buoy #5 but out of the channel. It was named for the surrounding property owner's daughter, who loved to fish here in the 1700s. Today shallow-draft bass boats venture in for the same sport Abigail enjoyed 200 years ago, and ospreys and medium-size blue herons and white herons nest here and catch carp. In the winter, bald eagles do the fishing. There is a small red icehouse on the shoreline of Abigail's Hole that the present owner uses for a skat-

The old house perched at the top of the steep slope on the east side of Abigail's Hole where it joins the Cove's Lower Bay is thought to have been built in 1690 by (or for) Elijah Ely. The entire mouth of the Cove can be seen from here.

ing house. The high surrounding hills provide protection from winter winds, and together with the shallow water depth make the place an ideal ice-skating "pond."

Just past Green Can Buoy #7 opposite the large red colonial-era home said to have been built around 1690, Hamburg Cove widens into the deep Lower Bay with a hundred or so mooring buoys. These moorings are privately owned and are registered with the harbormaster (no mooring may be placed without first being registered). There is really not room enough to anchor here, and it is best to pick up one of Cove Landing Marina's fifteen rental moorings, which are marked and painted bright orange. It is the harbormaster's policy that vacant moorings can be picked up by transient boats in lieu of anchoring. If the owner's boat returns, however, the mooring must be politely and promptly relinquished. Except on weekends, there are usually enough vacancies to handle the demand.

There is a no-wake-six-miles-per-hour speed limit in the entire Cove, and water-skiers and jet skiers are not welcomed. All vessels with an installed toilet must have a Coast Guard certified Marine Sanitation Device (MSD) attached to the toilet, and direct discharge to the Cove is illegal. Random checks for compliance are conducted by the harbormaster. The Cove Landing Marina in the Upper Bay has a pump-out facility for holding tanks.

Thanks to the efforts of all who use it, the water in the Cove gets cleaner every year. In 1992, the bottom was clearly visible along the shoreline, and empty beer cans and other jetsam were no longer seen on the shore. Swimming is good, with the water temperature around 76 degrees in the summer. The tidal range in the Cove is two to three feet. When I had a water sample from the Lower Bay tested in August 1992, it showed only 1.2 percent salinity; however, a boat staying all summer in the Lower Bay without antifouling paint protection will have barnacles on its bottom by the end of the season.

Until 1957, there were no waterfront homes on the south shore of the Lower Bay from the Connecticut River to Flat Rock.

All this property was owned by just two families, Richard Cooper and Virginia and Jessie Morgan Jones. Between Flat Rock and the Upper Bay, there were only five homes plus Camp Claire. In 1957, Virginia and Jessie sold some of their waterfront land and the area has become "built up." Actually, there are fewer than a dozen homes, most of them on high ground back from the shoreline so that they remain partially hidden from view by the trees.

Along the south shore of the Lower Bay is a freshwater spring that oozes through the sand at low tide. The Indians probably used it and marked and protected it with stones, some of which remain. My home is on this part of the waterfront. When I talked with one of the old-timers back in 1970, he told me that his primary chore every Saturday in the late 1890s was to row his boat to this spring to get his family's weekly supply of drinking and cooking water. An article about the Connecticut River in one of the yachting magazines in the 1920s described the spring as a favorite place for boatmen to replenish their fresh water. About twenty-five years ago, a wooden barrel was still partially buried in the spring, and clean, cold spring water could be bailed out at low tide. The old barrel has long since disintegrated, but the outline of its position is still marked by rocks.

Evidence of Indian occupation in the Eight Mile River drainage area dates back 4000 to 5000 years, according to Dr. John Pfeiffer, an archaeologist who lives in Old Lyme and has excavated sites throughout southeastern Connecticut. At first a nomadic society of hunters and gatherers, this area's Indians evolved distinct settlements of fifteen to twenty people 2000 to 4000 years ago. Eight hundred to 1000 years ago, they settled down even more with the advent of agriculture—corn, beans and squash. But they still fished for shellfish, alewives, shad, and sturgeon; still gathered berries and nuts, and hunted deer, bear, moose, and other mammals. Colonial records document a traditional hunting ground of the Western Nehantics as being south of the upper extent of the Eight Mile River. Apparently after contact with Europeans, small family groups lived in the river drainages from spring through fall, then moved inland to valleys sheltered from winter winds, bringing with them a larder of food including nuts, dried beans and corn, dried meat, even dried lobster.

All the Indians of southeastern Connecticut between Waterford and Madison/Guilford were probably interrelated small groups like this—Indians the Europeans identified as Niantic or Nehantic. Pfeiffer thinks that contact with Europeans—explorers, fur traders, fishermen—before 1600 introduced common European diseases like measles, whooping cough, chicken pox and smallpox with devastating effect. A Niantic Indian group in this area, he estimates, lost as much as 98 percent of its population to these diseases by 1600. In the beginning of the 1600s, there might have been 300 Indians left in what is now Lyme and Old Lyme. Evidence of seventeenth-century contact with Europeans includes a 1570 site on Joshuatown Road where clay pipes, brass and copper arrow points, and a rifle's flintlock have been found.

Hamburg Cove's Lower Bay, about two-thirds of a nautical mile long, narrows at the top and enters the midsection of the "lazy eight," with the Camp Claire waterfront on the south and a hillside of hemlocks on the north shore. In the late 1930s, a man named Tom Tracy, who commuted to Boston and New York in a seaplane, built himself a house overlooking this passage between the bays. The house was a one-of-a-kind structure built of logs. On the end facing the water, it had an open-end airplane hangar into which Tom could winch his seaplane. Various people owned or rented this house during the ensuing years and added wings, levels and other modifications, but the hangar with a propeller nailed across the peak of the room remained. One year the entire senior class of the Old Lyme High School had a party there. In 1990, this "landmark" between the Lower and Upper bays was torn down except for the chimney, around which the new owner has built a large contemporary house. Every now and then a seaplane still lands in the Lower Bay, and after taxiing around a bit to see the sights, takes off.

A narrow, winding channel marked by stakes starting with #11

The Lower Bay as painted by Hugh de Haven from the home of the late Robert Fiske. The painting shows the Cove just after the sun has set behind the Essex hills. deHaven also did an almost exactly similar companion painting in early morning. Acrylic on board. COLLECTION OF THE LATE ROBERT FISKE.

at Flat Rock leads to the Upper Bay and the tiny village of Hamburg. Although sizable boats can negotiate this channel, it must be carefully followed, and skippers not familiar with the passage and carrying draft of more than 6½ feet should not try it at low tide. There is a 6½ foot spot off the Hamburg Cove Yacht Club. Hug the north shore as you move through the Narrows, and after passing Red Nun #12, you will see the Upper Bay with its yacht club and two small, tidy marinas (but stay in the channel!).

The Hamburg Cove Yacht Club was founded in 1946, and its distinctive orange burgee has flown over the Upper Bay since 1963 when the present clubhouse property was acquired. The club maintains a dinghy float in shallow water where visiting yachtsmen can temporarily leave small boats and walk to the village.

Hamburg has been a genuine seaport for more than 150 years.

In 1827, the Eight Mile River Channel Company was founded to make the Cove navigable from the Connecticut River to the little village. With twenty initial stockholders, the company had various obstructions and shoals dug out to provide access for vessels drawing up to 9 feet. The owners charged a toll for passing up and down this route, and the rates ranged from one dollar for a vessel drawing 4½ feet to "two dollars twelve and a half cents"[7] for the maximum. It is not clear, despite far-ranging and freewheeling research, when the channels in Hamburg Cove were last dredged, but I was told by an old-timer that he thought it was in 1909. In the early 1930s, people living and doing business along the Cove asked the Town of Lyme for funds to dredge the channel again, but were turned down flat in a strident town meeting.

Even after the first dredging, passage through the Cove could be difficult for large vessels, such as the two coasting schooners in the Richard Brooks painting on page 119, because they had to be guided carefully through the narrow, winding channel to the Upper Bay. They would normally enter the Cove on an incoming tide and depart on the outgoing tide with the crew using long poles to guide and push the ships around the channel turns. If the breeze was fair and light, sails were used to ease the polers' work, but the sails had to be handled skillfully to prevent a sudden puff of wind from pushing the ship out of the channel.

Just to the south of the yacht club is a bridge where Falls Brook enters the Cove. This bridge is the focal point for the annual Lyme Fourth of July parade and "tea party." It is fun to pass under the bridge in a dinghy or canoe to explore the brook, which also passes under Hamburg Road (Route 156). Falls Brook was the source of water power for mills located in the Sterling City area of Lyme (the earliest established in 1710).

The town of Lyme owns a small parcel of land between the yacht club and the bridge which is used as a public launching area for small boats. There are five or six public parking spaces on Cove Road.

The best place to turn a boat around in the Upper Bay is

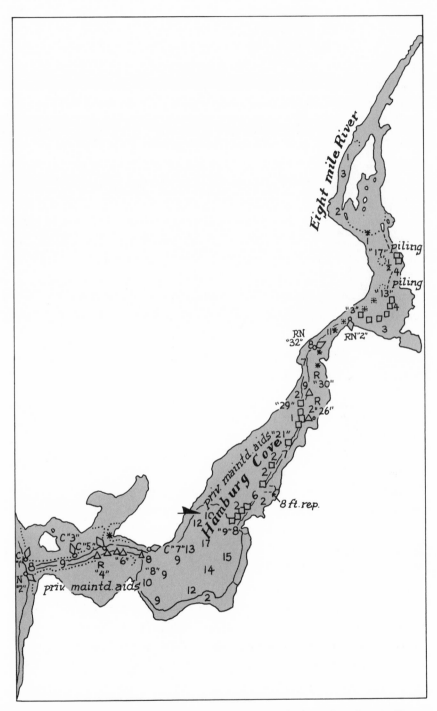

Copy of NOAA Chart No. 12375, showing water depths and markers in Hamburg Cove.

between the last channel marker and the south end of Cove Landing Marina. The site of this marina is where Joseph Lord in the early 1800s built a long bulkhead out into the water and filled it to make a flat landing area. Through the decades it had a variety of names such as Lord's Dock, Brockway Dock, Ephraim Reynolds' Dock, and just plain Hamburg Dock. In the early 1940s, the marina's owners, Lagel and DeSaulnier, gave it the name Cove Landing, and the present owner, John Leonard, has kept it.

Cove Landing Marina provides daily, monthly, and seasonal dockage and general repairs. It has a travelift to haul or launch boats up to 80 feet in length, 8½ foot draft, and 35 tons weight. The marina has a pumpout facility, a small ship's store, and block and cube ice, and provides electrical/mechanical repair and painting services for both sail and powerboats. Cove Landing specializes in the repair and restoration of wooden boats and can provide overland boat transportation as well.

At the end of Cove Landing's driveway and just to the left on Hamburg Road is a charming country general store, H.L. Reynolds Company. It has been in continuous business since it was opened in 1859. The locals call it "Jane's" (for Jane DeWolf, the proprietor since 1953). A visit to the store is a must for visitors, if not for basic groceries, beer, ice, etc., then to see the collection of original paintings by local artists that are for sale, the old photos and town memorabilia, the tag-sale items in the back of the store, and the most complete inventory of dollhouse miniatures and supplies in the state. If that is not enough, Jane is the best source of information on the history and present goings-on in the area.

Just across the road from Jane's is the Lyme Public Hall, the Lyme Congregational Church (Sunday service 10 A.M.), and the Grange Hall, which is the site of the annual Hamburg Fair in the middle of August. North of the general store is Reynolds' Garage and Marina, a service garage, auto dealership, and, on the waterfront, a small marina with large boat-storage sheds. The Reynolds' Marina has limited dockage in season but can haul and provide inside winter storage for about thirty small-to-medium-size boats.

The navigable portion of the Cove ends just past the Reynolds' waterfront. Beyond this to the Old Hamburg (Joshuatown) Bridge, where the Eight Mile River meets the tide, the water is deep enough only for dinghies and canoes—and even they may ground at low tide. But the area is one of the loveliest Hamburg Cove has to offer, and several of the most charming old houses in Lyme line the banks of the rapidly narrowing waterway.

≈

ROBERT B. GUSTAFSON, *following graduation from the U.S. Naval Academy, spent 27 years in the United States Submarine Service. He retired as captain. He has lived on the shore of Hamburg Cove since 1966.*

JOSEPH GRIBBINS *is director of publications for Mystic Seaport. He was formerly editor of* Nautical Quarterly *and has written extensively. He lives in Lyme.*

~ III ~

THE SURROUNDING COUNTRY

by JOHN H. NOYES

T he picturesque setting of Hamburg Cove and the surrounding country is a composite of attractive topography—of rolling hills, brooks, rivers, rock outcrops, and vegetation. It is a land of "edges"—separations between fields, forests, watercourses, and roads—and therein lies much of its beauty. The area radiates peace, but a peace that has often been hard earned by generations of quiet people working the soil, woods, and waters.

It has been said that the Eight Mile River—the correct name for Hamburg Cove—is like a fjord; and since fjords are rare in the United States, one may wonder how and when did this one come to be. What were its geologic origins? What was the role of glaciation? How have soils and climate influenced the vegetation?

One might even ask where Hamburg Cove was located 250 million years ago when "North America was part of that super continent, Pangaea—a land mass which included North and South America, Africa, Eurasia, India, Australia and Antarctica".[1]

For the answers to these questions, we must go back millions of years to the time when massive earth movements resulted in the faulting and fracturing of bedrock, which, in turn, determined where valleys are now located.

Eight Mile River is such a bedrock valley, cutting through Precambrian rocks some 600 million years old. Originally the valley was deeper, but over time it was filled in considerably by glacial meltwater deposits. Examination of the flatter and rolling lands near the Cove—around Cove Road, Ely's Ferry Road and Hamburg itself—indicates the presence of glacial deposits of sand, gravel, and clay along with pebbles and boulders of all sizes. These glacial soils have been augmented by the disintegration of rocks into fine material through the excretion of plant acids and the mechanical effects of roots, along with the accumulation of humus as plants and animals died and decomposed. The bedrock over which this mantle of glacial till rests is, in places, fifty feet below sea level.

Hamburg Cove, one of the most beautiful and protected small-boat harbors on the Eastern seaboard, is of very recent geologic origin. To understand the sequence of events leading to its formation, we need go no farther than Long Island Sound.

The great North American ice sheet that covered millions of square miles of land about 20 to 25,000 years ago was, in this locality of the Sound, at least a mile thick. Because a tremendous amount of water was tied up as ice, the sea level was 300 feet lower than at present, and the ocean was far-distant from Long Island and the mainland coast.

The southern edge of the ice sheet covered Long Island. There it stopped moving and became stagnant. As temperatures rose, the glacial-melt laid down deposits of sand, gravel, and rocks that formed a ridge, called a terminal moraine, the entire length of Long Island. The Sound itself, at the time of the glacier, was a basin, which, as the glacier melted, became a repository for both ice and water, eventually turning into a large freshwater lake dammed by the terminal moraine. When the melt-water reached a critical level, the lake broke through its dam in the vicinity of the Race, between the eastern tip of Long Island and Fishers

Island. Finally, about 15,000 years ago, the glacial melt raised the sea level enough to begin to enter the Sound and flood the lower coastal land.

As recently as 4000 years ago, there was still no Hamburg Cove—just the Eight Mile River valley, the lower extremities of which had been filled with sand and gravel deposits to a depth of fifty to sixty feet. In time the gradual melting of glacial ice to the north caused the sea to flood into the lower reaches of the valley, broadening the water surface there sufficiently to form the Cove as we know it now.[2]

The Forest

By the time Indians inhabited the Cove area, "climatic warming transform[ed] southern New England from the glacial tundra of 12,500 years ago to a series of forests composed in turn of spruce, white pine, and finally, by about 7000 years ago, the oaks and other hardwoods typical of the forest today."[3] Primeval forests are often thought of as pristine places untouched by man; but that is not always the case, because the Indians of southern New England burned many parcels of land to create a more varied habitat for game, improve visibility for hunting, and clear land for their villages and crops, especially corn and beans.

The primeval forest is an association of old-growth, dominant trees. It develops in stages of plant succession into a "climax" forest. Few examples of a climax forest exist, however, because of interruptions in the growth cycle. Fire, insects, and diseases, hurricanes, ice storms, and timber harvesting are setbacks that cause forests to start anew.

There are plenty of examples of plant succession that illustrate how forests evolve from open fields and abandoned farmlands. First-invaders are frequently coarse grasses, goldenrod, milkweed, thistles, bracken fern, greenbrier, poison ivy, Asiatic bittersweet, and honeysuckle. These plants give way to, or share the land with, shrubs such as barberry, bayberry, blueberry, and wild rose. The

Eastern hemlocks grew luxuriantly, to great height and in great numbers, around Hamburg Cove until the arrival in 1985 of the wooly adelgid. This dense stand on the shore of Abigail's Hole was one of the last to survive the insects' attack.

first tree species to become established in the succession include gray birch, pin and black cherry, honeylocust, red cedar, sassafras, sumac, and scrub oak. Finally, trees with longer life-spans—those of the red and white oak groups, beech, black and yellow birch, sugar maple, hickory, yellow poplar, pitch pine, and hemlock—become established as dominant species.

The many species of vegetation that are found around Hamburg Cove are influenced by soil, water, and climatic conditions. Fortunately, the Cove is in a temperate zone with forty to forty-five inches of precipitation quite evenly distributed throughout the year and a growing season of approximately six and a half months.

Early settlers were very observant people who took into account "the nature and diversity of an area's soils which might be crucial to the future prosperity of a new settlement, determining the success or failure of its agriculture. Colonists studied the native trees carefully for indications of soil fertility."[4] Pitch pine, for example, usually grows on lighter, less fertile soils not well suited to agricultural crops, while most hardwoods—the broadleaf trees—indicate a richer loam or loamy sand.

There is an unusually large assortment of tree species in southern Connecticut because we are in a transition zone between the northern forest and the central hardwood forest, and trees from both regions are intermingled. Trees of the northern forest that grow here include basswood, beech, sugar maple, and yellow birch; those of the central hardwood region include black birch, black gum (Pepperidge), hickories, the red and white oaks, yellow popular (Whitewood), and pitch pine. The American chestnut, once so common here, belongs in the latter group. A few trees such as white ash, black cherry, hemlock, red (swamp) maple, and white pine do not belong in either group.

Farming

Land clearing reached its height in Lyme about 1850. However, the transition from a land mostly forested to a land mostly farmed and back again to a land mostly forested was gradual, probably because, in a coastal community, there were numerous ways for a man to make a living—he was not entirely dependent on lumbering or farming. Nevertheless, during much of the nineteenth century, agriculture was the backbone of Lyme's economy.

An interesting description of agricultural activities in the area is found in the unpublished memoirs of Joshua Warren Stark, who

A typical Lyme farming scene in the eighteenth, nineteenth and twentieth centuries. Boulders and small rocks turned up by plows were built into stone fences or, if there was no need for a fence, simply accumulated in huge piles. POSTCARD, COLLECTION OF MICHAEL LLOYD.

was born in Lyme in 1862 and became its first selectman many years later. Stark's earliest recollection was of the growing of sorghum and its processing at a sorghum mill owned by Gigeon Rogers on Beaver Brook Road. Stalks of sorghum were run between rollers of a clothes-wringer-type press powered by a yoke of oxen on a sweep. The juice was then evaporated to a heavy consistency like molasses and used in place of it. When Puerto Rican molasses, imported in hogsheads, became plentiful and cheap, production of local sorghum ceased.

Stark also recalled that the country was covered with apple trees. Some of the fruit was shipped out, but most was made into cider for drinking and vinegar. Cider mills were common, and the cider they dispensed by the barrel had a going price of five cents a gallon.

When Stark was a small boy, nearly every farm had sheep. The popular breed was Merino because of the very high quality of the wool. At that time, little if any lamb or mutton was eaten, but later other breeds were introduced—Southdowns, Dorsets, and Cotswolds—and a taste for lamb developed.

Because so many sheep were raised in the area, a number of mills sprang up to process their wool. One of these was a fulling mill in Sterling City. Others were scattered around Lyme and Old Lyme—wherever there was a good source of water power, and where the mills could be easily reached by the rather extensive system of trails and roads that crisscrossed the region. These included the Rathbun Fulling Mill on the Eight Mile River north of Hamburg Cove; John Bradbury's scouring mill and textile mill (the latter purchased from Oliver Lay) on Mill Brook in Old Lyme; and the Clement Forsdick Carding Mill on Beaver Brook in Lyme.

Although sheep farming was an important business for Lyme farmers, commercial dairy farming was not until Leon Czikowsky settled on what is now known as Czikowsky's Hill towering over Hamburg Cove. Later, about 1940, the Tiffanys on Hamburg Road at the southern end of Sterling City Road entered the business and today run the larger of the two dairy farms left in Lyme. (The other is owned by J. Ely Harding on Bill Hill Road. The Czikowskys have been out of business for many years.)

In the period before herds of milk cows came on the scene, the only bovines present in sizable numbers were the oxen used for all hauling purposes and the steers that were raised for the market and to feed the farmers themselves.

The farmer's existence was precarious. Joshua Warren Stark recalled that in the autumn of 1884 when he first rented his Uncle Nathan's farm at $100 a year, "I felt I needed a horse first of anything, so one morning I started for New London on foot. I hated to do it, as I had not walked any for a year and was pretty soft, but father did not offer to help me out, and I would not ask him. I bought a cheap horse that afternoon—about $35 I think. I then went up town and bought a harness, put it on the horse, and started home. I got there about nine o'clock and was so tired that I went to bed without eating my supper. I then bought a yoke of oxen from Austin Riggs for $160 [during the Civil War, a similar yoke cost $300]. I bought about ten head of other cattle and a flock of sheep, farming tools, cart, chains, etc. It took all the money I had earned and also the $225 from my mother's estate which I had just come into possession of. I worked alone mostly the first year. Father and I changed work during haying. There was practically no income from the farm. I worked out some and hoped to be in a position to raise and sell a yoke of oxen a year at $150, a veal calf or two at from five to six cents a pound, perhaps some twenty lambs at $3 each, wool for about $20, and some cord wood on Hamburg dock at $3 a cord. Taxes were about $40."

By hard work, Stark improved his life considerably as time passed, but in all likelihood, he was unusual. Before he was born, a number of Lyme people that ultimately included Champions, Hardings, Huntleys, Lords, Marvins, Noyeses, and Pecks began to move westward. Their main reason for doing so was that the Lyme land was worn out, but there were other reasons: Following Connecticut's ceding of claims to land in the Northwest Territory, rich farmland in the Western Reserve was made available to Connecticut residents at the bargain price of six shillings per acre. Then came the discovery of gold in California; and if you didn't tap the mother lode, you could always stay on as a farmer or market-hunter. Then in 1862, the Federal Government's Homestead Act in effect gave a quarter section of land (160 acres) to almost anyone of legal age who asked for it. At the same time, westward migration was being facilitated first by the Erie Canal and other canals like it and then by railroads eager to span the continent.

So starting some time after 1850, the open land surrounding Hamburg Cove (and throughout the town of Lyme) began to revert to forest. Prior to that date, two-thirds of Connecticut had been cleared for agriculture. Today, two-thirds of the state is forested, and except for occasional apple trees that remain growing

Field over Hamburg Cove *by George Bruestle (1872-1939) clearly depicts one of the problems facing early farmers: rock underlying and bursting through the soil. Oil on canvas.* COLLECTION OF THE LYME PUBLIC LIBRARY.

in the woods, the only things left to show that the land was once farmed are the miles and miles of stone walls that were built for fences and to mark boundaries and simply to get rid of boulders turned up by plows.

Lumbering

The cutting of timber and its conversion into various products has a long history. Contrary to popular belief, early settlers in New England did not build log houses. Once they finally felt established in this harsh, strange land, however, they began to build substantial homes that required large timbers. Small logs with one flat side were used for roof rafters, purlins, and floor joists. Big logs with two, three, or four flat sides were used for sills, posts, and beams.

Tools for squaring timber were simple—a conventional axe (also called a narrow, falling or pole axe), a broad axe, and an adze. A board the width of the desired timber was placed along the length of a log to be hewed, and a sharp instrument called a "scratcher" was drawn along both edges of the board to mark the log. A chalk line was also used, especially on long logs. With an axe, notches were cut every eight inches or so along the log to the depth of the scratched lines, and the wood between the notches was chipped out. A broad axe was then used to smooth the two log faces. For extra-fine smoothing, the adze was used. When the two faces had been completed, the log was turned and the process repeated. Ship timbers were fashioned in the same manner.

An early method of cutting smooth-sided timbers, planks, and boards was to place a log on a platform constructed over a pit. One person stood in the pit; a second, on the platform above. Grasping the ends of a two-man saw, they ripped the log lengthwise. Hard work!

The first sawmills in the Cove area were water-powered. In the early 1700s Daniel Sterling established a sawmill on Falls Brook in Sterling City. Another mill, owned by Amos Tinker, was located on the Eight Mile River.

These early mills had a vertical "up-and-down" saw rather than a circular one. In this type of mill, a saw blade six to seven feet long and about eight inches wide was secured within a wooden frame that was water-powered to move straight up and down. Water power was also geared to pull the log carriage and log slowly through the moving saw. An old saying attests that sawing speed left much to be desired in this kind of mill: "Set the log for the thickness of board to be sawed, engage the saw, set the saw carriage in motion, go have your lunch, come back, take off the board and set the works for the next cut." Boards and timbers cut by vertical-moving saws can be identified by the right-angle saw-kerf marks on them. Such marks are found on many of the boards in Lyme's old buildings. Circular-saw kerfs are arc-shaped.

Water-powered mills were, of course, permanently located, so logs had to be transported to them; but mills located near rivers had the advantage that logs could be floated in from distant points for processing. Otherwise, logs were skidded out of the woods, loaded on wagons, and hauled overland to a mill. In 1861, a road to the Eight Mile River was approved by the Town of Lyme so that logs could be hauled to the mill there. This road started near the upper bridge over the Lieutenant River, crossed Saunders Hollow Road to a now-abandoned road to Bill Hill, then continued to Hamburg Road and Sterling City.[5] The commercial value of lumber in those days is indicated by such a road-building project.

Wood products from local sawmills were important to the economic welfare of a good number of Lyme's citizens. In addition to material for homes and local shipyards, lumber was cut for furniture, farm tools, and barrel staves. Staves, made of white oak, were an important item in the export trade to the West Indies. Barrels were put together during the voyage to give the cooper work and to make sure that the barrels were tight enough to ship rum back to Connecticut without loss.

With the advent of steam, portable mills replaced most of the water-powered ones. "In the late 1880s the steam tractor made sawmills portable. This tractor consisted of a railroad-type boiler with a steam engine mounted on top and the whole assembly mounted on two sets of large, wide-tired, iron wheels. The whole contraption was self-propelled and the engine, belted to pulleys connected to a circular saw, made a portable sawmill."[6] These portable mills revolutionized the logging and milling industry. The

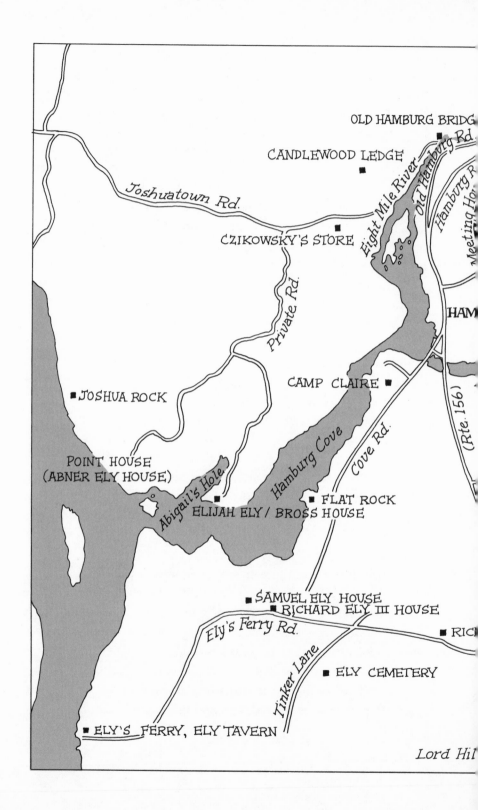

NDING)

Nickerson Hill

City Rd.

Fulling Mill Brook

Sterling Hill Road

NG.

Y

rchMill

Rd.

HOUSE

This is the Hamburg Cove area about which this book is written. It measures roughly two-and-a-half miles square. Hamburg Road (Route 156) runs almost due north and south up to where it splits off from Old Hamburg Road.

sawmill went to the woodlot instead of logs being hauled out of the woods to a mill miles away.

In later years, gasoline engines replaced the bulky hard-to-maneuver steam tractors. Sawmills were still taken into woodlots, set up, and run by gasoline-powered engines.

In the past thirty to forty years, however, the sawmilling business has come full circle; large, efficient, automated mills are permanently located with all the ancillary equipment of log debarkers, edgers, cut-off saws, and conveyor belts. Huge logging trucks now haul logs from the forest to the mill for distances of fifty miles and more. Occasionally you see one leaving the Hamburg Cove area with a load of great hemlock logs or a collection of mixed hardwoods from the forest back of Sterling City. They are proof that Lyme changes with the times. But it can also revert to old ways.

Not long before Leon Tiffany Jr. was killed on a hunting trip to Alaska, a friend of mine saw him hewing logs with a broad axe. He wanted them for a house he was building high behind his farm. He used a taut chalked line rather than a scratcher to mark his cut. Then, standing on or beside the log, he cut along the line with his axe until he had produced a flat, beautifully textured surface. The year was 1980, but Leon was producing construction timbers as his long-ago ancestors had done.

Over the past three centuries, the occupancy and use of land around Hamburg Cove have changed. The decrease in farming has resulted in a re-clothing of the land with trees. The Tiffany farm is a good example of how so much of the land was used years ago, but now the large land holdings have been reduced in size—inherited by or deeded to family members or sold to others.

The smaller, present-day properties are owned for a variety of reasons: for the pride of owning a home in a beautiful rural setting; for privacy from near neighbors; for a view of or access to the water.

In reality, the land has not changed. It is there. If it's not growing corn or hay, it's growing trees or is occupied by houses.

But people's values about the land have changed—from those centered on making a living from it to those focused around a non-agricultural life style. Hamburg Cove and its surrounding area adapt to both.

Important Trees of the Cove Area

When you walk or ride on the back roads around Hamburg Cove today, the aura of earlier days is strong. The forest has once again taken back the land, and the roadsides are a tangle of lesser vegetation providing habitat for many species of birds and mammals. There are fine vistas, framed by beautiful trees, of open meadows, a bedrock ledge, a tumbling stream, or a distant hill.

At least sixty species of trees are common to the Cove area. Here are a few of those that have been, and in some cases still are, of special interest to local residents:

Flowering Dogwood

Botanists will remind us that the four white dogwood "petals" are not really petals, but bracts. In any case, the native dogwood in full bloom is a beautiful small tree. It grows along roadsides and in woodlands, in openings, and under partial shade.

The wood is very hard, takes a smooth finish, and sustains repeated and sudden shock. Because of its strength, it was used in the South, where dogwood grows especially abundantly, to make shuttles for New England textile mills. The wood was so valuable that it was sold by the pound, which is probably the reason why plastic has now replaced it in shuttle manufacture.

In the fall, the attractive, bright red dogwood berries provide food for many birds and mammals; however, they are poisonous to humans.

This tree has suffered from a blight—an anthracnose-type fungus—that withers leaves and has killed a lot of trees in this part of Connecticut. Some recovery has occurred in the past several years, however. This is mostly in trees growing in the open, where better air circulation and sunlight discourage the moisture-dependent fungus.

Pitch Pine

Pitch pine, sometimes called scrub pine, grows on dry, light-textured soils. It is not plentiful, but neither is it uncommon in the Cove area. Its wood, as the name implies, has a very high resin content, making the wood durable and decay resistant. Some of the early settlers used pitch pine for sill and framing purposes in their homes and for decking and planking in shipbuilding.

Perhaps the most unusual local use for pitch pines growing near the Cove is mentioned by Marguerite Allis in her book, *Connecticut River*. She writes: "Candlewood Ledge [which is off Joshuatown Road at the north end of the Cove] gets its name from the pitch pine formerly cut there by thrifty folk eager to save tallow tapers." Called "lightwood," the pine was split into pencil-size or larger splinters twelve to fourteen inches long and used as candles or for lighting fires. Tapers and kindling made from the heartwood of the yellow or "hard" pines of the South are in common use today.

(Current evidence to the contrary, white pine is not indigenous to the Connecticut coastal area. The species was introduced here by man, and since then, has spread largely by self-seeding. Although our ancestors had many uses for the wood, they got it from logs floated down rivers from northern New England.)

Shagbark Hickory

Shagbark hickory is the most common of the several species of hickory growing in Connecticut. The wood is hard and tough, used for axe and other tool handles, wheels and spokes of farm wagons, and for smoking meat. The wood has a higher heat value per unit of volume than any other species in our woods. Hickory nuts have been a delicacy for years, hard to shell, but worth it. A mature tree may produce two to three bushels of nuts a year.

A rather specialized use for tall, slender hickory trees six to eight inches in diameter was for fish weir poles. The poles were driven into the bottom of Long Island Sound in a row at right angles to the shore, and netting, weighted along the bottom edge, was tied to them. Fish swimming toward the netting were diverted by it into a fish trap at the shore end of the net.

Dock pilings were made from trees of larger size. In the days of wooden barrels, hickory was the favorite wood for making barrel hoops.

Yellow Poplar

The local names for yellow poplar are "tulip tree"—because of its beautiful yellowish-green, tuliplike spring flowers—and "whitewood," because of its light-colored wood. This tree grows to large size even though it is near the northern limit of its range. Its natural form is tall and straight. The wood is easily worked, and I'm sure that Ephraim Reynolds used it in his carriage and wagon manufacturing business in Hamburg in the later 1850s. Many early homes were paneled with yellow poplar. It was also used for pattern and furniture making.

Black Gum

Black gum, locally called Pepperidge, is found most commonly in moist areas along rivers and streams, although it will grow on drier sites. It is one of the earliest trees to change color in the fall, turning a deep, shiny red.

In the days when horse-drawn wagons and carriages were the principal means of transportation, black gum was used to make wagon wheel hubs. The wood has a close, interlocking grain, tough and hard to split; consequently, it was perfect for securing the spokes driven into it.

Farther south, where black gum is more plentiful, the wood is used in the manufacture of furniture, flooring, fruit and vegetable baskets, crates, slack cooperage, pulpwood, and veneers. The tree produces plumlike fruits relished by many bird species.

Eastern Red Cedar

Eastern red cedar, which is not really a cedar but a juniper, is one of the first trees to invade abandoned fields and sometimes establishes itself in very dense stands. The early settler recognized the value of the tree for its many uses—as fence posts and shingles because of its durability; for lining chests and closets because of its fragrance, which also repels moths; and for building cabins and the superstructure of boats. Many people still use cedars for Christmas trees.

Red cedar is a good soil stabilizer. It is very important to wildlife, providing excellent nesting habitat and shelter for a number of birds. The cedar berries are eaten by cedar waxwings, wild turkeys, ruffed grouse, rabbits, and other animals.

Witch Hazel

The witch hazel is not classed as a tree. It is, rather, a large, coarse shrub, the wood of which yielded an extract used as a lotion, astringent, and cleanser. The Indians considered the extract a medicine and passed along their knowledge of it to early settlers.

In the 1800s, witch hazel was chopped at two mills on Sterling City Road. The chips were then hauled to the E.E. Dickinson Company plant in Essex for distillation. The company still makes witch hazel, but today it is a synthetic.

Witch hazel is an interesting plant. It flowers in late autumn, and when one year's flowers appear, those of the previous year are just ripening. The mature, hard, brown seeds are ejected from their casings with such force that some fly twenty to thirty feet through the air—a different way for nature to perpetuate the species.

Black Birch

Black birch, sometimes known as Sweet Birch, is a common tree in Lyme. It is found especially on lower slopes. The wood is used for flooring, furniture, woodenware, interior trim, and fuel. Small branches and saplings were also used in the past to manufacture oil-of-birch, more commonly known as oil-of-wintergreen, because it was made originally from wintergreen berries. Birch branches were chipped and distilled to make the oil, which was used to flavor candy and medicines. Supplying birch brush for the two mills in Sterling City provided income for local people. Today, oil-of-wintergreen is made synthetically.

Eastern Hemlock

Eastern, or Canadian, hemlock has fallen on hard times in southern Connecticut, and especially on the banks of Hamburg Cove, where it grew naturally in such profusion and to such height that one homeowner felt it necessary to cut down all his hemlocks in order to get more light into his house. Now an insect called the Hemlock Wooly Adelgid is doing to the remaining hemlocks around the Cove (and elsewhere in Lyme and Old Lyme) what this homeowner accomplished with a saw.

The wooly adelgid was first discovered in Connecticut in 1985 and is thought to have been blown across Long Island Sound from the island by Hurricane Gloria. It is covered by a white, cottony mass, and once it attaches itself to hemlock twigs, it just sits there, immobile, piercing the bark and sucking out the sap. Trees may die within a year, but more commonly, in three to four. Interestingly, this same adelgid was found in Oregon on Western hemlock in 1924, but that species of hemlock is quite resistant to it.

Controlling the insect is difficult, costly, and practically impossible in forest stands. The best control is with chemical sprays, the least toxic being an insecticidal oil or soap, but to be effective, the spray must cover the insect—and that is hard to accomplish in the dense stands of sixty- to eighty-foot trees that edge Hamburg Cove.

A further threat to the Cove area and Connecticut hemlocks is posed by five other insect pests. Fortunately, none of these is so dangerous hereabouts as the adelgid, but the outlook for the hemlocks is obviously not bright. If the species survives, it will be because of some insect parasite, pathogen, or predator.[7]

If the Eastern hemlock does not survive, Connecticut will lose one of its most beautiful, widely used landscaping, timber, and windbreak trees. Deer, turkey, and ruffed grouse will lose a favorite cover, and builders will lose an excellent material for framing and roof boards. I know of one Old Lyme barn, still sound, with hemlock roof boards 250 years old. Happily, as long as the trees last, hemlock wood can be used for rough construction, pallets, and in some areas, pulpwood.

Sugar Maple

Sugar maple, also called hard maple and rock maple, is best known for its magnificent display of fall colors. The gorgeous reds and yellows of this spectacular tree have attracted tourists and artists to the Cove for many years. It is one of the most common street and specimen trees in the Northeast, valued for shade and landscaping.

The wood of the sugar maple is prized for making furniture, flooring, and woodenware, and lumber with bird's eye or curly grain is worth its weight in gold.

Maple syrup is fast approaching similar economic value because the demand increases year by year; on the other hand, stands of sugar maple do not increase at the same pace, and it still takes about thirty-five gallons of sap to make one gallon of syrup. In days gone by, there were undoubtedly some Lyme property owners who engaged in collecting and boiling down sugar maple sap as a way of augmenting their incomes. Today, whatever "sugaring" is done in Lyme is done on a small scale and mainly to satisfy the participant's own sweet tooth.

White Oak

White oak is among the most valuable and sought-after trees in the area. During the years when wooden-boat building was a major business, white oak had special qualities that made it useful for marine use. It is a strong, close-grained wood, and when properly dried, very durable. Because of its unique cell structure, it is well adapted for below-waterline purposes in boat and ship construction. The wood cells are filled with tyloses that prevent the movement of water through them. White oak was by far the best wood for ships' keels, stems, ribs, knees, and rudders.

Another important use for white oak, because of its cell structure, was for making "tight" cooperage staves for barrels used in the West Indies rum trade: it was important that rum arrived back here without leaking. Whiskey casks and whale-oil hogsheads also had to be made of white oak. Barrels made from other wood species are termed "slack" cooperage and are used only for shipping dry products.

White oak was also preferred for the framing members in old houses and bridges and for making railroad ties, farm wagons and tools, furniture, and flooring. The acorns provide valuable food for squirrels and deer and for wild turkeys that are once again appearing in this region.

Today, as in early times, white oaks are dominant in the woods and fields surrounding Hamburg Cove. Although many are only a few score years old, they are tall, sturdy, proud trees, but even they pale and give homage to the handful of old-timers scattered around the country. These are Olympian trees. Magnificent beyond description.

The oldest of them all—indeed the oldest living thing of any kind in the Hamburg Cove area—is the white oak that grows near the right rear corner of the Samuel Ely house on Ely's Ferry Road. The various experts who have looked at it and tended it put its age at approximately 500 years. It is a superb tree with a massive, though short, trunk (oaks growing in the open tend to

The great white oak behind the Samuel Ely house is estimated to be 500 years of age—the oldest living thing in the Hamburg Cove area. Although the largest of the outstretched limbs have been guyed by wire, the tree was damaged by storms in 1992.

have much shorter trunks than those in the forest) and an enormous crown; in fact, the mighty limbs spread so far that recent owners have felt it wise to guy them with cables to prevent—but not always successfully— breakage in ice storms and hurricanes. We can only imagine what major and minor events have taken place under and around the old tree in its lifetime. There surely were many.

≈

JOHN H. NOYES *is a professor emeritus of the Department of Forestry and Wildlife Management at the University of Massachusetts. A native of Old Lyme, he is an eighth generation descendant of Richard Ely I and the seventh generation from the Reverend Moses Noyes, first pastor of Old Lyme's First Congregational Church.*

~ IV ~

THROUGH
ARTISTS' EYES

by PAMELA G. BOND

Since the turn of the century, attracted by tales of the signal beauty of the place, American artists have found their way to Hamburg Cove. Many came from the artist's colony at Old Lyme; others from Hartford, New York, even Chicago; all were awed and delighted by the myriad facets of a cove nestled like a jewel in its handsome setting. Seeking to capture the Cove's infinite variety on canvas, its shallow waters reflecting the hills and every nuance of the sky, its exuberant celebrations of the seasons, the artists left behind hundreds of impressions of Hamburg Cove, each as individual as the brush that painted it.

Some of the artists settled in Hamburg and painted their views of the Cove again and again from the hillsides, the shores, the water, from windows and boats and Old Hamburg (Joshuatown) Bridge, immortalizing a site that is very little changed today. The pictures, like all paintings by Old Lyme colony artists, sold well from the start. The first exhibition was organized in 1902 at Old Lyme's Phoebe Griffin Noyes Library, where similar shows were held every summer thereafter until 1920, when the artists inaugurated their own Lyme Art Association Gallery. Using their New York connections, the confident artists persuaded the *New York Times* art critic to review the first couple of shows and, from then on, no persuasion was needed. The early canvases of Hamburg Cove are now widely dispersed: sold and resold over the years, prices rising with the artists' prestige, they grace collections all over the United States. Very few remain in this area and it is these few—with the permission of their owners—that illustrate this chapter.

Hamburg Cove has never lost its magic for the artist. Contemporary painters still set up their easels on rises overlooking the 8-shaped Cove, cope with palettes in rocking boats, or sketch the scene from Cove Landing—but their numbers have dwindled. Today's painters have to supplement precarious incomes with year-round jobs. In those halcyon days, from the turn of the century until World War II, artists could afford to devote their lives to art, particularly if—as implied by a very old gentleman who knew the Cove painters of that era—they'd had the foresight to marry a wealthy woman. (From the number who did, it is clear that marriage to a respectable artist was considered a desirable match.)

The American Impressionists were not the first to discover Hamburg Cove; George Francis Bottum, a notable artist, was on the scene in 1840, commissioned by Mr. Reed (his first name is unknown) to paint *Reed's Landing*. The painting, once owned by Judge William Marvin, was given to the Town of Lyme by Marvin's widow. It shows, unmistakably, the Eight Mile River and the Old Hamburg Bridge. The grass landing is still there, as well as most of the houses, the red barn that is now a house, and the section of Old Hamburg Road that crosses the bridge to become Joshuatown Road. (See front cover.)

Bottum painted at least two copies of *Reed's Landing* (photography being unavailable) but left the copies unsigned. He is a bit of a mystery: although the painting hanging in the Lyme Town Hall is clearly signed "G. F. Bottum, 1840," most of the sparse bio-

Hamburg Cove *by Charles H. Ebert (1873-1959) shows the Upper Bay and Czikowsky's Hill in 1930. Oil on board.* Museum of Fine Arts, Springfield, Mass. Gift of Anne Rogin.

graphic material on this artist refers to him as "Bottume." He became a popular portrait painter, and it is probable that Bottum was considered an indelicate name in the early part of the nineteenth century (particularly by the ladies) and was rendered less offensive—by others if not by the artist himself—by gallicizing its pronunciation. He is cited in the venerable Benezit's *Dictionaire Des*

Peintres, Sculpteurs, Dessinateurs Et Graveurs as G. F. Bottume, born in Baltic, Connecticut in 1828 and deceased in Norwich, Connecticut in 1846. These dates are repeated, and the *e* added to the name, in a new American Artists biographical dictionary, but the erroneous information was obviously taken from Benezit. It is hard enough to believe that the wondrous *Reed's Landing* was painted when G. F. Bottum was 12, but impossible to credit that he studied art in Norwich, traveled about, painted and made copies of large landscapes of Salem center and a Salem farm, not to mention Lyme and Hamburg Cove, *and* became "well-known for his portraits on Connecticut's eastern shore" if, as Benezit claims, he died at the age of 18.

An excerpt from H. W. French's *Art and Artists in Connecticut*, found glued to the back of *Reed's Landing*, solves part of the mystery. It says George F. Bottum went to New York to study at 13, but "was obliged to spend" the first three years "under Albertson, a sign-painter in Norwich, where he died on March 27, 1846." Mr. French's haphazard syntax would lead one to conclude that it was Bottum who died, but further reading shows it was Albertson who passed on in 1846. G. F. Bottum, according to French, was still alive in Springfield, Massachusetts, in 1879, when *Art and Artists* went to print.

Bertram Bruestle painted the same Old Hamburg Bridge (Page 67) sometime before 1938, when it was replaced by the prettier bowed version we have today. It is interesting to note that the State of Connecticut, faced with the necessity of building a new bridge after the 1938 hurricane, asked Hamburg artists to submit design suggestions, though specifying construction in wrought iron or cement.

George Bruestle (Page 37), Bertram's father, was probably the first of the American Impressionists to summer in Hamburg Cove. Soon after his return from France, at the turn of the century, he bought a small place that had once housed Hamburg's Masonic Temple on its second floor. George Bruestle spent all but the coldest months there (the house was not heated) until the end of his life. Bertram studied under his father. He ground his own paints as his father had learned to do in Europe and attended Lyme schools when the family returned to Hamburg Cove before the end of the school year. Away from the city for much of his early life, Bertram developed an intense love of nature. He became not only a fine painter but also one of the first nature-film makers—the films and his hundreds of drawings and slides are now in the Thames Science Center in New London. George Bruestle left the house in Hamburg Cove to Bertram; it still stands, just south of the west end of Old Hamburg Bridge, the name "Bruestle" proudly lettered on the mailbox.

Next door to the Bruestle home is the onetime home and studio of Egbert Cadmus, a successful New York lithographer and watercolorist, married to an illustrator, and father of Paul Cadmus, who became a far more famous artist than his father. Egbert spent his summers in the area, according to one of the old-time neighbors, "Painting every red building in sight." George Bruestle, confined to his home one day, looked out the window of his studio and rendered a lovely pastel sketch of Cadmus' quite ordinary barn and shed and outhouse.

Some years later James Goodwin McManus bought the house on the other side of Bruestle's and encouraged his students from the Connecticut League of Art Students—he taught at night there for years—to come down on Mondays and "paint the countryside." Monday was the day Mrs. Magee hung out the wash from the balcony at the front of her house on Old Hamburg Road. Under McManus's tutoring eye, the students set up their easels and daubed on canvas their impressions of the flapping lines of color on the other side of Reed's Landing. Egbert Cadmus and his wife, whose sensibilities were offended by displays of drying laundry, took day trips every Monday, returning only after everything had been taken in.

It was McManus who introduced Albertus Eugene Jones (a colleague and fellow prizewinner at the Connecticut Association of Fine Art) to summers in Hamburg Cove. He may not have meant to, but one year McManus asked Bert Jones to drive him down in his car. Enchanted by the place, Jones bought a surplus World War I boat, rechristened it *Natoya*, and moored it in the Cove (Page 118). He lived on it with his wife every summer, seldom pulling up anchor but painting scores of watercolors from the vantage point of his deck. He went ashore to paint Hamburg Cove children when he was preparing oils for exhibitions in Hartford. Many residents remember posing for Jones and other painters, sitting still as mice until dismissed with a pocketful of candy.

Charles Vezin (Page 69), a New York artist who had stayed at Miss Florence's in Old Lyme—he painted the city scene on one of the dining room panels—fell in love with the tranquility of Hamburg Cove. In the early 1920s, he rented a 1739 saltbox that still stands on Czikowsky's Hill. Vezin was entranced by the Cove's changing light; he endeavored to capture the changes by painting a scene shortly after daylight and again in the late afternoon.

Oscar Fehrer was another artist captivated by the beauty of Hamburg Cove. He spent a summer with his family in the now much-enlarged house beyond the Cadmus place on Joshuatown Road. Possibly because his small daughter Catherine crossed the road, rolled down the bank, and tumbled into the Cove on the family's first day there, Fehrer bought a house on Beaver Brook Road, well removed from the water, the following year.

The best work produced by the painters in and around Hamburg Cove in those idyllic summers was shown (1902-19) in the Phoebe Griffin Noyes Library in Old Lyme—where the "regulars" at Miss Florence Griswold's boarding house had arranged to hold the art colony exhibits. Later, needing more space for the very popular exhibits, the artists built their own gallery on property deeded by Miss Florence and inaugurated it as the Lyme Art Association Gallery in 1920. Stimulated by rave reviews in the *New York Times* and conveyed from the railroad station directly to the gallery in a horse-drawn carriage, art lovers, dealers, decorators, and even museums came to add to their collections. It is doubtful whether Albertus Jones and James McManus, both teachers with no outside income, could have lived as comfortably as they did if not for gallery sales.

Either because large pictures are awkward to transport, or for simple economic reasons, some of the Hamburg artists exhibited small versions, or sketches, of the bigger pictures they hoped to sell. Will Taylor showed sketches of paintings he had already completed; others waited for the client's commission. The sketch was withdrawn, of course, when the larger canvas was acquired or commissioned, but not necessarily destroyed. The painter usually kept these in his studio as a record of his *oeuvre,* though after his death (when all artists' work becomes more valuable) a few of these sketches may have been sold as finished paintings.

Looking at it today, one can easily imagine the sun-washed Cove dotted with painters' easels, children watching curiously, cows standing warily, gulls wheeling overhead. Sometimes one can almost see the artists walking back along the winding roads after a pleasing session with the Muse, burdened with easels and palettes and wet paintings, stopping to compare notes with their fellows before going home to their waiting wives.

The wives, faced with the prospect of cooking hearty meals in country kitchens, usually opted for regular noonday dinners at Mrs. Martin's boarding house on Sterling City Road, near Reynolds' Boatyard. Leland Reynolds recalls George Bruestle's Model T Ford arriving every day at twelve, young Bertram in front beside his father, Mrs. Bruestle seated in the back. He also remembers Edward Rook, a wealthy man and notable mountain laurel painter, taking Mrs. Rook out for a spin in his Hupmobile on Saturday afternoons, driving as far as the end of the macadam at the church corner, and back again to Old Lyme. (Shortly afterwards, the talented but eccentric Rook gave up painting altogether in favor of collecting cars.) When the macadam paving was extended, Eugene Higgins—he painted Hamburg Cove but was better known as a member of the Ashcan School—felt compelled to give up his house at the corner of Beaver Brook Road. He and his wife were devout nudists, and the improved road threatened their privacy.

Competition threatened Mrs. Martin's "home-cooked meals, reasonable" when Miss Marguerite Slawson, an Indiana schoolteacher, bought Green Shadows, a Federal-style farmhouse on Route 156, and turned it into an inn. But by that time—1920—there was enough business for both. Miss Slawson even built three weekend studios to accommodate out-of-town artists. Faced with all this convenience, the artists' wives seldom lit their wood-burning kitchen stoves except for breakfast and light suppers and occasional hot baths. Bread, staples, and cheese—a gigantic wheel of cheddar—were available at Czikowsky's store; dairy products, eggs, bacon, and ham at nearby farms.

James McManus, unmarried, with no car and very little money, brought his sister down to keep house for him, but poor Miss McManus loathed the primitive conditions, the outhouses, the "terrible quiet," and the "dirty country store," and did not hesitate to say so. Fortunately, McManus's Hartford students often came to the rescue, driving down with supplies of cooked food or taking their desperate teacher out to dinner at Green Shadows.

Czikowsky's store was eventually razed, but not before the land it stood on had been immortalized by the painters of Hamburg Cove. The Czikowskys also did a thriving wholesale business, driving a horse-drawn rig loaded with meat and produce across the bridge and up Route 156 to Norwich every day (frequently providing short lifts to easel-toting artists). The family put its profits into farmland and accepted acreage from neighboring farmers in settlement of outstanding accounts.

Czikowsky's Hill, as it came to be called, rising high on the right of Joshuatown Road and overlooking the Upper Bay, was an immensely popular site for artists. Every American Impressionist for miles around painted Czikowsky's Hill, or from it, at one time or another—until someone inadvertently left a turpentine-soaked painting rag stuck in a crevice of a wall. A Czikowsky cow ate it and died, and the artists were no longer welcome.

The inadvertence of another, non-Impressionist painter of Hamburg Cove—Will S. Taylor (Page 91)—robbed us, and him, of several views of the area. He was burning a "batch" of his own paintings in the stove when a fellow artist dropped in, found him looking chagrined. "Wrong batch," Taylor said ruefully, indicating the ones he had intended to burn, unsatisfactory results of his constant experimenting with new art forms and techniques.

Taylor, who later joined the art department at Brown University and taught there for twenty years (Hamburg Cove residents still refer to him as Professor Taylor) built a summer house on land above Old Hamburg Bridge, reached by road from Route 156—opposite the old toll house—and by water from the Eight Mile River. For his daughter's wedding, he chose to fill the cottage with flowers of his own picking and enlisted the help of Sylvia Harding, who owned a canoe. Together they stripped every low-lying laurel on the Upper Bay, filling the canoe to overflowing and returning with the blossoms only minutes before the guests arrived. Taylor had asked Sylvia to do most of the picking because of his bad shoulder, the result of a fall from scaffolding while painting the twelve huge Indian murals in New York's Museum of Natural History. (The fall prompted his loving wife to take a tailoring course and, from then on, to weave material and tailor Will Taylor's jackets to fit his awkward shoulder.)

The mountain laurel was back again next spring, covering the banks and gentle slopes, exciting the painting instincts of every artist in the area. No one waited as eagerly as William Chadwick (Pages 60 and 65), who lived in Old Lyme and drove up every May to paint the short-lived profusion of blush-tinged white flowers, often using them to frame poetic springtime views of Hamburg Cove. He came again with every change of season and left a body of work that is a paean to the Cove. These paintings and the others he did were much admired by his fellows; and sometime after his death, dealers discovered his work and his reputation soared. His restored studio now stands on the grounds of the Florence Griswold Museum, transported there from Bailey Road, where it stood behind his handsome home.

Chadwick had spent several summers at Miss Florence's, where

Reynolds Boatyard, *now Reynolds Marina, in the Upper Bay. Oil on canvas by William Chadwick (1879-1962).* COLLECTION OF ELIZABETH CHADWICK O'CONNELL. PHOTO BY JOSEPH STANDART.

he met many of the artists who followed his example and established residence in Old Lyme's art colony. Among Miss Florence's boarders who bought houses on Lyme Street were Charles Ebert, George Brainard Burr, Winfield Scott Clime, Edward Rook, and Matilda Browne. It is amusing to note that some of Miss Florence's paying guests found Old Lyme "too busy," and complained of "too much traffic noise on Lyme Street"—in 1909!

Charles Ebert painted Hamburg Cove every year. He was an Impressionist in the strictest sense of the word. He painted exactly what his eye saw in a self-limited amount of time, and he did not add remembered embellishments later, in his studio, to round out the picture. Writers on painting agree that one of the hardest things for an artist is declaring a picture finished: there is always a touch here, a line there, an added spot of color. Ebert, as is evident in *Hamburg Cove* (Page 53) had no such problem.

Winfield Scott Clime (Page 107), who lived across Lyme Street from Ebert, painted Hamburg Cove from farmland on Huckleberry Hill. Another farm he often visited was Scott's apple orchard, on the Boston Post Road in East Lyme; his pictures were often on sale there in the apple and cider season. When Clime had dental problems, he found a good New London dentist who was willing to barter professional services for paintings. Retired now, that understanding dentist has a wallful of Clime's pictures to cheer his sunset years. Clime's studio still stands, across the driveway from the Old Lyme firehouse, but no artist has lived in the house since his death.

Except for the fact that he exhibited his oils and pastels regularly at the Art Gallery in Old Lyme and that his property extended into Old Lyme, Harold Saxton Burr had no direct connection with that town. He had inherited the Manse, an ancient house with an eccentric "hatted" tower on Town Woods Road in Lyme, from his father, who had inherited it from *his* mother, a direct descendant of Peter Lord, who had built the house. He lived there every summer while working as professor of neuroanatomy at Yale. Burr painted so enthusiastically that he found himself giving pictures away for lack of room to house them. While he painted, his wife undertook the monumental task of "translating" almost indecipherable Lyme Town Records into typewriter print.

Wilson Irvine (Page 63) was already a well-known Chicago artist when he began spending time in Hamburg in 1914. He bought a year-round home on Sterling City Road in 1918 and dedicated the rest of his life to painting the Connecticut countryside. A *plein-air* painter like his fellow Impressionists, he loved the outdoors; when it was too cold to stand outside, he painted whatever was visible from his windows and porch.

One of Irvine's special friends was Guy Carleton Wiggins, famous for his New York winter scenes. He bought an ancient yellow farmhouse on Route 156, across from Marguerite Slawson's property, and walked to Hamburg Cove to paint the summers. To cover the expense of the house, Wiggins started a painting school in his barn. When it burned down, he taught in his studio and let his students sleep in the attic.

Robert Vonnoh, also a friend of Irvine's, was a well established painter and teacher of Impressionism before he came to Lyme to spend summers with his second wife, even better-known sculptor Bessie Potter Vonnoh. They chose an area stretching along Beaver Brook Road and called Pleasant Valley. Vonnoh loved setting up his easel in some part of Hamburg Cove, painting all morning, joining other painters at Green Shadows or Mrs. Martin's, and returning to paint another view in the afternoon. Vonnoh began showing his work in Lyme Art Association exhibitions in 1917; his wife showed her sculpture there from 1916 on.

Another serious woman artist of that time (there were very few) was Gertrude Nason (Page 70), a part-time resident of Lyme and sister of Thomas Nason, the famous wood engraver. Gertrude spent six months of the year in New York—where she and her husband, William Donohue, shared a studio—and the rest of the time in a house she adored on Birch Mill Road, off Sterling City Road, in Lyme. Not much of a housekeeper, she lived for her art—and from it. When Thomas Nason (Page 111) built his house on Joshuatown Road in 1938, she learned wood engraving from him—but only in order to make the Christmas cards she later colored by hand, and a few Christmas sketches. Gertrude much preferred painting in oil, or sketching in crayon or colored pencil, but was unable to persuade Thomas away from his woodcuts. A master engraver, Thomas captured every aspect of the Cove in his stark black-and-white prints—but it was a less romantic Hamburg Cove than the one pictured by Hamburg painters. They saw the sunlight and shade on open fields, the sparkling water framed by laurel, the contrast of red barn on snow. Thomas Nason, later than most of the them, saw the failing farms and sagging buildings, the grueling work that went into maintaining a livelihood for farm families.

Winter over Hamburg Cove *by Wilson Irvine (1869-1936). As evidenced here, Lyme was largely unforested during Irvine's lifetime. Oil on canvas.* COLLECTION OF MR. AND MRS. RICHARD D. ROBERTS, NORFOLK, VA.

Gertrude Nason produced dozens of scenes of Hamburg. An enormous number of them have simply disappeared, though part of her work survives in the Public Library in Boston, where Gertrude began her career.

Margaret Miller Cooper, prolific painter and world traveler, was married to a wealthy man and painted wherever she went. She lived on Ely's Ferry Road in the old Samuel Ely home. When she died, her sons gave many of her pictures to the New Britain Museum of American Art and endowed a wing. Her *River Boats, Hamburg Cove* (Page 66) shows another face of that blessed place, known to all who seek safe anchorage after sailing the Connecticut River.

One notes wryly that Bruce Crane (Page 148), who mastered realism, turned tonalist in France, and went on to become an Impressionist, might never have become a painter at all if he hadn't stumbled "before a lot of young lady amateur painters" in the Adirondacks one summer: Their studies inspired him to pursue the painting career that led him to Miss Florence's in Old Lyme.

Impressionist Allen Butler Talcott conveyed the early-morning stillness of the Cove that is manifest even today, before summer sets in with its influx of visiting boats. Talcott bought a farmhouse on Neck Road (Route 156, south of Lyme) in 1903, after spending two summers in Old Lyme at the suggestion of Henry Ward Ranger, the artist who discovered Miss Florence Griswold's boarding house while searching for a Barbizon in America. Until his too-early death in 1908, Talcott shared his Talcott Farms studio with New York Art Students League colleague and well-known teacher, Frank DuMond, who later bought a year-round home on Grassy Hill Road.

For a view of commercial shipping in Hamburg Cove in 1906, we have Richard Brooks' canvas (Page 119) painted from a photograph. The docks shown, where lumber and barrel staves were loaded, are now Cove Landing, but little else except boat traffic has changed. The schooner pictured, the *Tansy Bitters*, is being poled through the shallow channel on an incoming tide.

Hamburg Cove *by William Chadwick (1879-1962). Mountain laurel grows luxuri-antly on the hills surrounding Hamburg Cove. This is a view of the Lower Bay and the Connecticut River beyond. Oil on canvas.* MUSEUM OF FINE ARTS, SPRINGFIELD, MASS. MUSE-UM PURCHASE.

River Boats, Hamburg Cove *by Margaret Miller Cooper (1874-1965) shows the Upper Bay and Czikowsky's Hill in 1935. Oil on canvas.* COLLECTION OF THE NEW BRITAIN MUSEUM OF AMERICAN ART, CONNECTICUT. GIFT OF THE ESTATE OF MARGARET COOPER. PHOTO BY MICHAEL AGEE.

Old Hamburg Bridge *by Bertram Bruestle (1902-1968). This was the bridge that crossed the Eight Mile River at Reed's Landing before it was rendered unsafe and unusable by the flood of 1936 and the hurricane of 1938. Oil on canvas.* COLLECTION OF THOMAS E. CATHCART, JR. PHOTO BY SKIP HINE.

Hamburg Cove *by Hugh de Haven (1895-1979). de Haven painted Hamburg Cove as well as the lower Connecticut River from every angle. Here he was looking across the Upper Bay toward the village of Hamburg and the First Congregational Church on the hill. Acrylic on board.* COLLECTION OF LELAND REYNOLDS. PHOTO BY SKIP HINE.

Hamburg Cove *by Charles Vezin (1858-1942) is actually of the Eight Mile River below Old Hamburg Bridge. Oil on canvas.* COLLECTION OF MR. AND MRS. SKIP HINE. PHOTO BY SKIP HINE.

House in Hamburg *by Gertrude Nason (1890-1968). The house, which no longer exists, was actually on Sterling City Road, near the artist's summer home on Birch Mill Road. Mixed media on paper.* Collection of Leland Reynolds. Photo by Skip Hine.

Hamburg Cove *by Roger Dennis. In the distance is Czikowsky's Hill. Although the Upper Bay does not become so crowded with boats as the Lower Bay, many are moored here in the summer. Oil on canvas.* COLLECTION OF THE LATE ROBERT FISKE. PHOTO BY JOSEPH STANDART.

Hamburg Cove. *The Upper Bay as seen by Muriel Reade Leeds from Czikowsky's Hill. Oil on canvas.* COLLECTION OF MRS. WILLIAM WEBSTER. PHOTO BY JOSEPH STANDART.

After loading, it had to wait for high tide before leaving the Cove. Brooks also painted a view from Czikowsky's Hill (Page iv).

Roger Dennis (Page 71), nearly as old as this century and personally acquainted with every artist mentioned here, except Bottum, is still painting and experimenting today. He began as a schoolboy in Norwich, where he received a scholarship for excellence in drawing at the Slater Hall School. For a very long time, he denied his desire to paint because oil paints were too expensive. He used to walk from New London and back to see the work of the Old Lyme artists and, in 1917, met Bertram Bruestle, when they were both fifteen. Bertram introduced him to his father and to Hamburg Cove, and Roger Dennis gave up drawing: the Cove's colors were too enticing and George Bruestle taught him how to mix his own paints. Later, Dennis took lessons from James McManus at the Connecticut League of Art Students, driving the lonely road from New London to Hartford every week. He was soon elected a member of the Lyme Art Association and, from then on, his fine pictures of Hamburg Cove, Old Lyme, Niantic beaches, Vermont, Maine, England, and his own and neighbors' gardens, have graced the association's member shows every year.

Hugh de Haven (Pages 23 and 68), who died in 1979 at the age of 84, painted miniaturized views of Hamburg Cove. A safety engineer by profession, he spent a large part of his career studying the effects of impacts on the human body. This led him to invent the seatbelt for automobiles. When he retired, he and his wife, a concert pianist, bought a house at the end of Brockway's Ferry Road and de Haven began to paint. He moored his elderly boat—which resembled a small version of the African Queen—at Reynolds' Marina and kept a dinghy on the tiny beach at the foot of his property. He soon knew every inch of Hamburg Cove and started many of his jewel-like compositions on the boat, finishing them on dry land, where he could wield a steadier brush.

In his Cove painting, non–Impressionist marine painter Charles R. Kinghan, presented an intimate, charmingly detailed version of the Upper Bay as it appeared when he visited Lyme in

1966. A noted watercolorist, Kinghan had recently returned from a journey to Great Britain and the Scottish Isles, commissioned by the U.S. Navy to paint U.S. Naval institutions there and the countryside around them. Those pictures, after a worldwide goodwill tour, now hang in the Smithsonian Institution in Washington, D.C.

Contemporary watercolorist Chet Reneson, a resident of Old Lyme, painted *The Secret Pool* (Page 77). This is on the Eight Mile River somewhere between Old Hamburg Bridge and the old Will Taylor property. Muriel Reade Leeds of Long Island (Page 72), painted her view from Czikowsky's Hill when she came up for a day in 1950 with a group of fellow artists. Bill Steeves, long a fixture on Lyme Street in Old Lyme, portrayed Old Hamburg Bridge in the 1970s. And Sultana Hanniford rendered her version of the Cove and its triple-arched bridge with a painstaking pallet knife. Beatrice Orchard-Todd, living on Sterling Hill Road in Lyme, pictured the Cove under ice in abstract color. Tom Torrenti, an Old Saybrook artist, became a familiar sight in the Cove area peering around his easel at the water and surrounding hills.

Today's artists are not as carefree as the early painters; the vast majority can only dedicate to painting the hours left over from earning a living. This chapter stands as a tribute to Hamburg Cove and that long ago time when the Lyme/Old Lyme art colony thrived; when artists rented houses and spent whole summers at the Cove; and the most pressing problem a *plein-air* painter faced was keeping the cows away from the turpentine.

~

PAMELA G. BOND *was born in England and lived all over the world before settling in Old Lyme in 1975. She has published translations of two novels and a book of poetry; written for publications in Bangkok and Vietnam; done an interview program on cable television in Mexico; had a play produced in New York; and been art critic for a Lower Connecticut River Valley newspaper. She recently completed her first novel.*

~ V ~

OF SHIPS AND SHAD

by CARLIN KINDILIEN

When I drove my pickup into the town landing on the eastern side of Old Hamburg Bridge, a young, black-bearded fellow was breaking down his spinning rod before his opened trunk. He did not turn, and I could tell that he was not having a day of days.

"Anything doing?" I asked as I stepped out.

"No," he said and then looked toward me and smiled. "But it's a nice spot."

I nodded. It was a handsome May morning, one of those days full of the prospect of warmth and revival. The shadblow bushes were in full white flower; the thick dogwood buds were about to burst. All around us mostly maples, some hickories, a willow, and white birch here and there were greening again.

"Have you fished here before?"

"First time. I was driving around last weekend, and I saw a man take a big brown trout right over by those rocks."

"Must have been a sea run. Right time. Just about everything is in here one time or another," I exaggerated.

The town landing is a demarcation line between fresh water

and tidal river. Here the Eight Mile River comes twisting down through a tunnel of dying hemlocks, makes a 90-degree turn just above the bridge, and continues its snaky way through Old Hamburg, the Cove proper, and empties into the Connecticut River, eight miles above its mouth at Long Island Sound. At low tide, the area around the landing is more mudflat than stream, but this morning the tide was still rising, and the water was high and turbulent after some recent heavy rain.

"You might do better upriver today," I suggested. Since I had left my fishing gear at home, I was feeling generous.

"Where about?"

"I'd try back of the Lyme School." Trout must have been stocked there for opening day. "Go back to the main road," I pointed up Joshuatown Road toward Route 156, "turn left and go a mile or so to the second left, a road below the school. Go over the bridge and try the channel on the far side of the river."

Although he looked suspicious—maybe he thought I wanted his spot—he mumbled some thanks and drove away.

I went back to the pickup and began to untie my dented aluminum canoe, glancing now and then at the river. "River" may be a misleading tag, except during spring rains. A "narrow stream" or "wide brook" is more accurate for many places between this bridge and the headwaters to the northeast. Most of the Eight Mile River is bypassed by local fishermen. Our youngest son and I fished a stretch from Mazer's Bridge to the dam for ten years, from the time he was six until sixteen, and only three times did we share it with other fishermen.

I have had some exciting fishing hours: on a sweltering August morning along Florida's Indian River when the sea trout were rippling the surface as far as we could see; in Wyoming's Wind River when the tip of my fly rod broke and I tied it back on with a shoelace and had a furious skirmish with a cutthroat trout; and one drizzly morning in the deep waters of a Connecticut lake when I thought I had hooked a log until "it" began to run and at the moment of truth my line snapped. Yet without question, my

The Secret Pool *by Chet Reneson. Above Old Hamburg Bridge, the Eight Mile River is a wide rushing stream interrupted here and there by deadwaters. The state stocks it annually with trout. Watercolor.* COLLECTION OF CHIP BATES. PHOTO BY JOSEPH STANDART.

happiest and most consistently productive times have been spent casting to bass and pickerel in the coves and marshes, shallows and sunken trees of this Eight Mile River.

This morning, however, I had a more responsible mission than snagging a couple of chunky black bass for lunch. My assignment: to report on shipbuilding and fishing in Hamburg Cove. I have done my homework, pestered the reference librarians at the Connecticut River and Mystic Seaport museums, read many of the maritime histories of New England, blessed the ladies who deciphered and transcribed Lyme's town records, listened to the tape recollections of shad fishermen, interviewed a score of townspeople, and checked the fishing reports and forecasts in local papers and fishing magazines. Still, before I put any words on paper, I wanted to paddle once again from Old Hamburg (Joshuatown) Bridge to the Connecticut River and look and listen and remember.

I carried the canoe to the nearest bank, skirted a couple of boulders, and slid it into the water. I held it parallel to the shoreline, stepped in gingerly, knelt before the stern seat, and pushed away toward the bridge's middle arch. Hamburg Bridge was built in the later 1930s after the original 1759 wood structure was moved off its piers by flood waters in the 1936 storm. It would probably have floated far away if Ken Plimpton hadn't roped it to a tree. I drifted through the cool shade into the scene that delights me in every season: the narrow stretch of water between green and wooded banks and ahead the reed-covered island and the steep hillside where the river turns into the wide cove, Old Hamburg Road on the left and Joshuatown on the right, and the rows of old and new homes behind white fences and rock gardens, sprawls of yellow forsythia, and mounds of pink-tipped rhododendron buds.

At this point, I always long for a camera to try to capture what is a transient beauty. I have driven down Joshuatown Road, across the bridge and onto Old Hamburg Road hundreds of times in my daily commute in every season and have never been able to keep my eyes on the road ahead. I have relished this river scene in summer's long reflections, in autumn's wild display, in winter's icy frames, and on spring mornings like this one. Motionless in the canoe, I tried to imagine how an impressionist would "see" these sunny shafts and green shadows, how the watercolorist would fix on paper this edge between reality and reflection.

While today Old Hamburg is a serene and sedate suburb, only 150 years ago this area was known as Reed's Landing, and it was Lyme's busy commercial center. An itinerant painter, standing on the eastern bank and looking toward the bridge in 1840, recorded the earlier reality: the stores on each side of the bridge, the piles of lumber and crates waiting to be shipped, the scow and sailboat in the river. Lyme's first settlers were drawn here because this was the first place where the Eight Mile River was narrow and shallow enough to be easily crossed and eventually bridged. They built bulkheads of stone on each side of the landing as platforms from which their boats or barges could be loaded for river trade or later reloaded on larger ships for reshipment to distant ports.[1]

Early in the eighteenth century, sloops stopped regularly in river towns like Lyme with ever-increasing demands for goods. Lumber was an important early export. In 1708 the town granted Captain William Ely permission to transport 33,000 hogsheads and barrel staves from Lyme.[2] The West Indies trade had been established early on the Connecticut River, and after 1700 a routine traffic in such products as beef, horses, fish, and port was gathered in small vessels along the river to be reshipped at larger ports. The West Indies traders returned with molasses, sugar, and rum (which was beginning to challenge beer as the colonists' drink of choice). In time Lyme's shipping center shifted to Hamburg's loading docks in the Upper Bay, and this continued to be an important shipping point for a large area to the east throughout the nineteenth century. Often one hundred yoke of oxen crowded the docks to unload railroad ties and ship masts.[3]

To this day, tradition maintains that Reed's Landing included a shipbuilding yard in the eighteenth century; and if memory serves my neighbors well, ships were built in this cove well into the following century. "Oh, sure," one man told me, "they built all kinds of boats right alongside the bridge." Another pointed out the house where the shipyard's superintendent lived, and a lady recalled her father telling of his grandfather mentioning "when the whole meadow beyond the bridge was filled with a huge hull under construction." The late James E. Harding in his two books about Lyme saw a shipyard in Reed's Landing as a logical extension of William Sterling's sawmill operations in Sterling City. ("His sawmill was mainly to provide timbers for ship construction.") Jay

Harding dated the Sterling Shipyard from 1710 to 1778, located one of its skidways "right beside the eastern end of the bridge," and described the typical construction of a sloop.[4]

Maritime historians have been less certain about Hamburg Cove's shipbuilding heritage. David Ransom, an architectural historian, studied Old Hamburg/Reed's Landing for possible inclusion in the National Register of Historic Places and came away with "a sliver of doubt" that vessels of any size had ever been built there.[5] May Hall James does not mention any such shipyard in her comprehensive *Educational History of Old Lyme*[6] nor does Barbara Deitrick in *The Ancient Town of Lyme*,[7] although each pinpoints the yards at Brockway's Ferry and Hadlyme. Edmund Delaney does not refer to a Sterling Shipyard in his *Connecticut River*[8] nor does T. A. Stevens in his authoritative maritime history of Old Lyme. John V. Goff's exhaustive study of shipbuilding in the Connecticut River Valley follows Harding's account.[9] Robert Harvey, whose ancestors gave their name to Lyme's Harvey's Plains, is a resident expert in matters maritime at the Connecticut River Museum's library in Essex. He and I spent hours flipping through a fat file of ships built along the river and found no mention of a Sterling Shipyard or of any vessel built at Reed's Landing or in Hamburg Cove.

My canoe, on automatic pilot, entered the narrow channel below Sylvia Harding's hillside home. It was there that I decided, all evidence notwithstanding, that Jay Harding was probably right about vessels of some kind being built along the Eight Mile River. Why? Simply because Lyme's earliest settlers desperately needed scows and sloops, pinnaces and wherries if they were to travel on the two rivers, their prime links to the outside world; and the only way to get one quickly was to build it themselves.

A Lyme farmer or tradesman contemplating his first boat had plenty of incentive. Shipbuilding along the Connecticut River began in 1648 when Thomas Deming, a Boston shipwright, came to Wethersfield and built the *Tyrall* for the West Indies trade. By 1680 the Hartford Colony of 12,000 people had twenty-seven vessels in the seagoing trade. John Tinker began to build vessels at Essex in 1720, and shipbuilders in Haddam constructed a brig as early as 1734. Before 1850, 4,000 vessels had been built in the lower river valley, and forty-five shipbuilding yards have been identified and documented. From 1784 to 1888, 200 vessels for coastal and foreign trade were launched from four yards in Lyme and Old Lyme. "In Essex," John Goff wrote of this time, "there wasn't a backyard but had a skeleton craft on the stocks." Lyme men must have heard the sounds of whipsaw, adze, and caulking mallets on all sides.

Anyone who writes of colonial shipbuilding—including me and our one-time good neighbor on Cove Road, Jay Harding—needs a robust imagination. Colonial records on the subject are quite wanting. There are references to small craft of the ship's boat class—the shallop, skiff, and pinnace (this was the first type of ship built by the English in America in 1607)—yet just what these vessels were in hull design and rig has been the despair of maritime historians. While scores of small boats were developed to work in local water and weather throughout North America, their histories are obscure. R. G. Albion reminds us in his *New England and the Sea* that contemporary observers were seldom interested in a "poor fisherman's boat."[10]

Vessels built at Reed's Landing must have been quite small, probably no more than forty or fifty feet, and shallow in draft, because at low tide there are only a few feet of water in this part of the Eight Mile River. Certainly, Lyme needed shoal draft boats for its rivers and coves. The earliest ferries on the Connecticut River were canoes and flatboats; and flat-bottomed scows and long boats were popular throughout the coastal colonies. The early designs must have taken into account the special requirements of the Connecticut River. Only tall masts with plenty of topsail would hold the wind in the river's sheltered coves and bends. Size was another important consideration, because flood tides were often not strong enough to carry boats upstream against the current, and they had to be hauled with ropes from shore.

Lyme had all the basic necessities for shipbuilding: manpower, materials, and construction techniques. A couple of handy men—the same men who were putting up houses and barns—could build a boat of some kind. Scows, punts, skiffs, and sharpies with their flat bottoms are the easiest to build and require the fewest tools and least time, especially when they are constructed "by guess and by God," without plans. Wood was easily come by—southern pine, white pine, white cedar, or white oak (depending on the size of the vessel) for hull; white pine for masts—and once the sawmill was operating, the whole building process accelerated dramatically.

Obviously, the larger the vessel, the greater the skills and coordination required for complex tasks. But even here, the amateur colonial shipbuilder was not working in totally uncharted waters. Construction techniques of more sophisticated craft have changed little since the seventeenth century, according to Howard I. Chappelle in his *American Small Sailing Craft*. A Swedish shipbuilding book published in 1691 (and reprinted in 1943) includes detailed plans for a shallop, a twenty-foot-long boat with two masts of a type popular in colonial America. One plate shows how these shallops were built on stocks on which the keel was erected with stem and stern and transom in place. In addition, five complete molds or forms (cross-sections of the hull) are shown. The Swedish setup is much like what is still seen in yards that build traditional small boats, yachts, and larger vessels in wood, and the tools and equipment are quite similar to today's hand tools.[11] Such a building method must have been common along the Connecticut River in the eighteenth and nineteenth centuries.

Lyme's two major shipyards at Brockway's Ferry and the Comstock yard in Hadlyme built large sailing vessels in complex operations involving the manual and skilled labor of as many as fifty carpenters, joiners, and caulkers. Carpenters hewed planks and shaped spars—all the processes that went into making a rough hull. Their prime tools were saw, adze, auger, and mallet. In 1802, one carpenter was paid three shillings per 100 for the 2300 treenails he fashioned for one vessel. Because of the amount of hammering they had to do, caulkers had the most grueling work with their caulking irons and mallets to make the hull and deck waterproof with oakum and tar. Ship joiners, the elite of the trades, used a collection of saws and planes for their finishing work on rails, deck structures, and cabins.

After the War of 1812, shipbuilding declined along the Connecticut River, and by 1850, the day of the wooden ship was about to end. Steam and steel would now dominate the river, and in our century, pleasure craft with inboard and outboard engines became more and more common, marinas and yacht clubs appeared in the coves once occupied by building yards and loading docks. Lyme/Old Lyme birth records of 1847-56 listed the occupations of the parents; these included 118 farmers, two book publishers, and only one boat builder.

The birth records also listed two fishermen. Maybe only two full-timers were busy in Lyme, but I bet there were many, many amateurs who on occasion wandered off with rod and net. About the fishing potential of the Eight Mile River as it makes its way through the Cove, I have no reservations. While boats may or may not have slid down skidways along Reed's Landing, as sure as "the Lord made shad," fish have long been found in these waters in impressive numbers.

Perhaps I do have some selfish reservations in reporting on these fishing grounds. Fishermen, I hope, will never throng to the banks of the Eight Mile River as they do at Latimer Brook in Flanders or below the Connecticut River dam in Enfield, just below the Massachusetts line. Little danger of that, I suppose, since fishermen are driven by herd instincts that seldom lead them to the coves of the big river. In these often lakelike environments, a prodigious quantity of game and coarse fish live out their life cycles in that crossroad where fresh water meets salt. Yellow perch, catfish, panfish, and eels have been caught in these coves in commercial lots for years. Smallmouth and largemouth bass, pickerel, shad, and brown trout are all here for the catching as they have been since man first sought food in Lyme's waters.

In the centuries before the English arrived, the inshore American waters, from the polar regions to the tropics, teemed with enormous numbers of anadromous fish like shad and salmon that return to rivers to spawn. Early-on fishermen tell of seine nets being torn from their grasp by massive schools of shad. Fish brought Europeans to these waters in the first place, and fishing became New England's first industry. Although most of Lyme's settlers were farmers, they were well aware of the special bonus awaiting them in the nearby rivers: A farmhand could easily match his annual salary with a couple of months shadding—and have some fun in the bargain.

The Indians chose wisely when they settled in Connecticut in one of their densest concentrations in North America. This rocky land of rivers, lakes, streams, marshes, and forests abounded with wild berries and nuts, shellfish, deer and foxes, bear and wild turkey, and fish of many kinds. Long before the Europeans arrived, the American Indian had developed some clever techniques and devices to catch fish. Some brooks were so packed that an Indian could quietly approach a docile fish, gently stroke its underbelly, and, once the fish was pleasantly hypnotized, toss it on the bank. More conventionally, the river Indians used hooks of wood, bone, clams, and shells; basketry traps, pounds and weirs made of wild hemp; and spears that some angling historians think were the first fishing poles. White men found the Eastern Indians tying the same knots that European fishermen used for their gill and seine nets. Surely, the arrivals could not improve on the design of the Indians' fishing boat, the birchbark canoe. At night the Indians speared fish from their canoes, holding torches high to silhouette their targets against the sandy bottom. The torches also attracted small panfish that inevitably lured larger species within spear range.[12] Chief Attawanhood, who later took the Christian name of Joshua, lived on a ridge between the Eight Mile and Connecticut rivers and had a special stone seat in what is now called Joshua Rock, from which he could watch all the fishing activities of his Western Nehantics.

Historic records of the seventeenth and eighteenth centuries contain few facts about the fishing resources of the Connecticut River. Salmon are rarely mentioned, causing some to wonder if they might have been less numerous than we now assume. Salmon nets appeared on the river before 1700; and although salmon were salted in casks for family use, they were seldom sold in the marketplace. After the first dam was built at South Hadley in 1795, few salmon were caught.

A *History of Middlesex, Connecticut* (1819) notes that shad "were caught plentifully in many places in Connecticut before 1760, and were sold at one penny and one-and-a-half pence some years later. They were carried away on horses. Thousands of barrels of shad were put up in Connecticut for troops from 1778 to 1781." Timothy Dwight wrote in 1812, "Since salmon left [the Connecticut River], it is frequented by great numbers of striped bass." [13] Lyme's waters were particularly rich: One fisherman reported catching 3,000 striped bass in a single March day in 1820.

Fish were so numerous in the Connecticut River and its tributaries that laws to regulate fishing were not needed for a long time. Bruce Stark writes in his history of Lyme that as late as 1753, Lyme fishermen, using nets or seines, were each year taking out of the Eight Mile River 200 barrels of small fish in addition to large numbers of shad and striped bass. A controversy developed when Charles Phelps stretched a net across the mouth of the river where it flows into the Connecticut. When catches dropped dramatically—from twenty barrels a year to two for Thomson Miller—the upriver landowners led by Daniel Ely petitioned the General Assembly to prohibit any obstructions across the river three-quarters of a mile from its mouth. In 1755 the Assembly passed responsibility for regulating the Eight Mile River to the New London County Court, and this court prohibited fishing "below the elm tree" on Timothy Tiffany's land but allowed Tiffany the right to fish on his own land. Arguments continued until the General Assembly took back the right to regulate fishing on this river and in 1770 forbade anyone to fish below the elm tree while giving Tiffany permission to use seines from Monday to Friday. Tiffany became a full-time fisherman, specializing in alewives for shipment to the West Indies.[14]

A couple of hundred-plus years later, I lingered in my canoe along the shaded shoreline below Sylvia Harding's white house halfway up Joshuatown Road's first hill. When Sylvia was a child, it was called Jared Daniels' Hill after her father. His obituary writers remembered Jared Daniels as the dean of Connecticut's fur traders: his business stationery carried his trademark—a drawing of a skunk with the caption, "Looking for Daniels: He will sort me right." He was also a schoolteacher, a cattle breeder, a farmer, constable, selectman, tax collector, an enthusiastic participant in Lyme's town meetings, and each spring and summer for sixty-five of his eighty-five years, a commercial fisherman from the flat landing below his home. In 1930 Will Taylor painted a charming portrait of Daniels' fishing operation on this spot with its ice house, tin shed, a stack of "fish cars" (holding tanks), the long boathouse, and Jared's three fishing boats. Today, only the boathouse remains.

Men like Jared Daniels, men who were born shortly after the Civil War and reached their prime in the new century, saw the schooners' last sail, the heyday of the steamboat, and the end of big-time shad fishing on the Connecticut River. Robert Huey fished the river for more than fifty years. Will Hall taught George LaPlace the winds and tides, they launched their boats from many sites in Lyme, notably Hamburg Cove and Brockway's Ferry, and they fished every reach in the lower river. They—Fritz and George Czikowsky, Wells Halleck Martin, Joe Rand, Phil Sands, Everett Beckwith—held other jobs as farmers, merchants, shipbuilders, hunters, and trappers and became full-timers only when the shad were running. The turn-of-the-century postcards catch them at work, repairing and drying their nets, loading their boats, readying for another long night on the river.

Spring returns to Lyme each year sometime in April when the shadbush blooms in its white clusters, shadflies dart in the

The huge linen nets used by early Hamburg Cove fishermen were mended and dried in the sun every day after the boats returned to the Upper Bay. POSTCARD, CONNECTICUT RIVER MUSEUM.

warming sun, and the silvery, splashing shad come back to the Connecticut River where they were spawned four or five years before. They are completing a still mysterious migration that has taken them through the deepest canyons of the Atlantic to our southern shores and then instinctively north with the rising temperature to this river. Just as shad have been doing since men first watched from these banks.

Probably the very abundance of shad led the colonists to take it for granted, even scorn it. For some, shad eaters revealed "a deficiency of port and destitution," and in one Old Saybrook church, shad eaters were required to sit apart from the rest of the congregation.[15] Another drawback was that shad had to be eaten with great caution unless its 1,500 bones had been removed or boiled away. Even today, fishermen remember when they fished only for roe shad and used bucks (males) for lobster bait. Not until early in this century was a way to bone shad deftly and quickly finally worked out. An expert hand—and there are fewer and fewer each year—is still needed for the thirty-two different steps required to slice out each string of tiny, overlapping, Y-shaped bones with just enough flesh to hold the bone structure intact.[16]

Nevertheless, by the end of the Revolutionary War, shad fishing had become a profitable enterprise, and Yankee ingenuity was about to move into a highly exploitative mode. Stone piers ("fish places") began to loom into the river from both shores. Often these were just a dump of rocks big enough to hold a platform and a capstan for hauling nets. A small boat paid out a seine net on an incoming tide and then drew it back in a downriver sweep, making a loop and enclosing any fish that had run up against it. By 1818, more than eighty of these fish places lined the river as far north as Hartford.[17] Some were large-scale operations run like western ranches with bunkhouses and kitchens for the workers who lived on the piers during shad runs. In addition, by mid-century, forty to fifty gill nets were drift netting the river every night.[18]

This overfishing, along with, the 1849 construction of the Connecticut River dam at Holyoke, Massachusetts, brought the end of major commercial shad fishing on the Connecticut River. Some efforts at conservation, like the restocking program in the ponds on Joshua Creek below Brockway's Ferry Road, were innovative and successful, but the shad that returned hereafter were caught in two-man efforts.[19] And these have dwindled over the years. During the 1940s, two dozen boats usually fished a popular reach in the lower river; by 1980, only nine boats were turning out at sunset. From her home in Sterling City, Elizebeth Plimpton recalls the evening she realized "that I didn't hear any shad boats in the Cove, and that I hadn't heard any for a long time. You could always hear the engines puffing as they went out at dusk. That sound was as familiar in springtime as the Czikowsky boys calling their cows."

Thanks to Elizebeth Plimpton, we know a good deal about the shad fishermen from Hamburg Cove who almost disappeared after the second World War. Determined to preserve a rich local heritage, she organized a group of her Lyme neighbors—Elizabeth Putnam, Eleanor O'Connell, Sylvia Harding, Verne Hall, and Leon Czikowsky—to collect shad lore. They gathered such artifacts as nets and buoys; photographs, paintings, postcards, and documents; and taped the fishing recollections of Roon Tooker, Norris Joseph, and Allan Bartman. Much of this material has been turned over to the Connecticut River Museum and the Mystic Seaport Museum.[20]

Connecticut River drag boats, about sixteen feet long and six feet wide, were the choice of most shadders in the two-man operations. These boats usually had centerboards and were gaff-rigged with jibs; the boats were undecked because the net has to be worked over the stern. While Oliver LaPlace remembers racing other boats to the reaches, it was strictly oar-power during the drifts. In this century the lathrop, a one-cylinder engine, became the standard power source. Elizabeth Putnam says that this engine was called a "one-lunger" and had to be crankstarted. The most common boat used today for shadding is the Brockway scull—an open, sixteen- to twenty-foot plywood assembly—built by Earl Brockway in Old Saybrook.[21]

The typical shad net is almost a quarter of a mile long (1,200 feet) and twenty feet wide with diamond-shaped meshes of slightly more than five inches. These are gill nets that allow a shad to put its head through the mesh but not to withdraw. The net is marked off in six-foot sections, called "snappers," that are weighted at bottom and supported on the surface by cork floats. On each end of the net is an old-fashioned kerosene lamp, attached to larger floats, that is used to track the net and keep it perpendicular to the shore. Early nets were made of Irish linen or cotton; now they are nylon. LaPlace remembers his aunt weaving the linens on winter evenings. The top and bottom ropes were sometimes tarred, and Allan Bartman's nets were dyed red as was the bottom of his boat ("We tried every color, and red catches more fish"). Meshes could be customized in size to catch mostly the male bucks or the female roes. "Sinkers" were about two inches long and made of lead, and the oval-shaped floats were made of cedar or white pine, eight inches long, and painted white.

Two men, according to Elizabeth Putnam, could string a net in a couple of days. When they finished, the net was put on a big wooden reel or hung between two poles to await the new season. After every outing, any tears in the net were mended immediately, and the net was placed on poles, allowing it to dry horizontally. Linen nets dried in the sun; modern nylon nets are covered with canvas to protect them from the sun. Today, a nylon net costs about $1,000; Robert Huey paid $40 for his linen net in 1911.[22]

Drift netting, the technique still used by Connecticut River shad fishermen, just as it was by their fathers and grandfathers, sounds easy enough. The net is put across the river on an incoming tide and followed by a drag boat as it drifts upstream. At the end of a drift, an hour or two, the net is hauled aboard, and the fishermen remove the shad caught in the gill net that is less visible to shad at night.

But shad fishing is tedious, tough, and dangerous work carried out by eventually tired and irritable men in small boats. During the two-month-long run, they go out night after night in all kinds of weather into a black world where shore and water merge. They call their fishing areas "reaches," stretches of river a few miles long to which they have staked claim by repeated use. Old-timers, it is said, could fish their reach blindfolded. They knew every snag, every buoy where the net had to be taken up and over, "where the shad bunch." What they didn't know was

Jared Daniels' Fishing Operation *was painted by Will Taylor (1882-1968) in 1930. The boathouse is the only thing left. It is on the west bank of the Upper Bay toward its northern end. Oil on canvas.* COLLECTION OF MRS. SYLVIA HARDING.

when a steamboat—a diesel tug now—might bear down on them, when a floating tree might rip their net to shreds, or storm or wind might "push" the law of averages on night fishing. Allan Bartman described one early spring return to shore with six inches of snow in the bottom of the boat—and the boat trembling with his shivering. The year 1929 was difficult for stockbrokers and great for shadders: Bartman worked around the clock hauling big catches. He didn't take off his clothes from Sunday to Friday, and then he slept for 48 hours.[23]

Oliver LaPlace began fishing in the 1930s. He fished with Will Hall for seven years to learn the tides, winds, fogs, landmarks, bottoms, the peculiarities of every reach.

Allan Bartman caught 500 tons of shad in his fifty-two fishing years and maintained that there was a science to shad fishing. Long before the state started its tagging research, he marked shad in the Sound to see how and where they traveled. He claimed (and often proved) that he could release a marked fish in the Sound and catch it within eight hours. Bartman learned that shad move on the tide at certain times and temperatures, that fish follow the channels "like a flock of sheep"; that nets had to be set differently on every tide and most fish were caught on a slack tide, that "once we found a school, we stayed on it like seagulls"; and that the best shad are caught in the lower river "where they have just left the cold Atlantic Ocean and are still 'hard as a rock.'"[24]

In 1900, fishermen brought in 300 to 400 shad in a single night; since the 1930s, a catch of thirty to sixty is hoped for. Today shad fishermen take their haul directly to local markets; they can earn a few thousand dollars in a productive six weeks. In earlier days, they dropped off their catch on the Steamboat Dock in Essex for reshipment by steamer to New York, or the shad were packed in wooden boxes between layers of cracked ice and taken to Deep River to be entrained to the Fulton Fish Market in New York. Later the shad boxes were picked up in Lyme by trailer trucks. Allan Bartman had some prosperous years with "fast buck shad" and some grim ones: in 1944, he made $9,000; in 1921, he and his striker each cleared $50. Occasionally, there were windfalls. On June 15, 1917, Robert Huey and George LaPlace caught a nine-foot sturgeon in their shad net. They towed it to Hamburg Cove, and the Fulton Fish Market sent a packer and a truck for the caviar. Huey and LaPlace received $222.93 for that night's work.

Reluctantly, I left the shade of Jared Daniels' landing, glanced up at the four steel garden chairs lined up on Sylvia Harding's lawn high above, and paddled down the Cove past Jane's store, Reynolds' dock, and the Cove Landing Marina, and turned into the Lower Bay. For several very special years in the 1960s our family lived in a most remarkable house along this stretch of the river. Here Tom Tracy, an architect who commuted between New York and Boston by seaplane, built a twelve-room log cabin with an attached hangar. He used the cedar poles that were readily available after the hurricane of 1938 tore through the Cove. Tom Tracy's log house and hangar are gone now, but as I paddled by this morning, nothing blurred my memory of those happy days when we lived year round on this laurel-and-hemlock-covered shore. There is no better way, I am sure, to know the possibilities and pleasures of Hamburg Cove.

I began to fish seriously when I was well along in my middle age; the pressure to make up lost time was heavy throughout my apprenticeship, much of it served in these waters. Fortunately for me, I was in the right place because fishing is a year-round activity on the Cove. On the cold, gray days of early winter, I went after those green-bronze missiles called pickerel with light lines and lures. When the Cove froze, I chopped through the ice and dangled minnows before their long snouts. (Pickerel grow extra big in brackish waters.) In early March, the white perch began biting, and I had plenty of fishing companions, especially where Falls Brook enters the Cove. White perch, which are really olive to dark blackish-green in color, look like small striped bass and taste even better in chowder. While they chase worms and minnows on the bottom, we had our best luck casting small bass bugs and poppers in the early evening when the perch came to the surface to feed on insects.

Eeling is another productive year-round fishing activity on the Cove, although not for me. I never achieved much enthusiasm for this snakelike fish on the end of my line, although it was a rare outing on the Eight Mile River when we did not see an eel or

The Hangar House was built by an architect for the seaplane he used to commute to and from Hamburg Cove's Lower Bay. The author of this chapter and his family lived here for several years. The sketch is by his wife, Charlotte Kindilien.

three. Sylvia Harding tells me that men came regularly from New Haven to buy hundreds of pounds of her father's eels. Chamb Ferry speaks of a night in a Cove boathouse when he listened to a couple of eelers counting their night's catch and reaching 200 before he fell asleep. In winter, eelers search for eels in the mud with hooked poles. In spring and summer when eels are especially active, the pros watch the winds closely, because the right ones drive eels into shallow water where they can be netted or trapped in eel pots – wire barrels with entrances at both ends. In his Jordan Village (Waterford) barbershop, Jack Martin told me that one of his customers was expanding his Connecticut River eel business and airshipping them alive to meet a growing market in Japan.

I have never caught a shad in the Cove or anywhere else.

Fishing authorities of this region, however, report that it is easy fishing from mid-April to late June; and I have watched my neighbors pull in many a buck shad in the Cove with spinning tackle and red and white shad dart lures. This is surprising because shad are plankton feeders and should not be interested in lures. Moreover, they do not feed on anything during their spawning runs.[25] Whatever the reason—maybe they are angry or territorial—they snap at certain lures. Word along the Eight Mile River is that shad seek dark cover or deep holes and that the best fishing is mornings and evenings, notably on drizzly, dark days. I am still trying.

One of the fascinations in fishing Hamburg Cove is that this aquatic habitat satisfies such a range of fishing interests. When you cast a line in these waters, you should be braced for the unexpected. While it may not be a nine-foot sturgeon, it could very easily be a striped bass, a snapper blue, a rainbow, all kinds of panfish, or, as it was for a fellow casting from the Hamburg Bridge in May, a six-pound brown trout. Look for big channel catfish near weedbeds and for bullheads after dark, and remember that in the fall, white catfish are omnivorous in the Cove area.

My favorite target in the Cove and all along the Eight Mile River is largemouth or smallmouth bass. These fine game fish can be found everywhere with the best fishing in mid and late summer: the lower and warmer the river, the better the fishing. Bass will go for any bait it thinks is alive, and, once it is hooked, you can anticipate a magnificent aerial display.

And if the fish are hiding when you venture on these waters, you can find ample reward just by sitting back and taking a leisurely look around. If you are lucky enough to be out on a not-too-humid July afternoon, you might scan the shore for a wildflower called the Indian paintbrush. It's a softer red than the scarlet on the perch's fins. You will soon be aware of a whole spectrum of color in this little river world: the flat purple of swamp flowers, the brilliant yellows of water lilies in the summer sun, the full oranges and iridescent blues of the scattering sunfish, the white flashes from the slender wings of the patroling mockingbird, the endless shades of green leaves, and the crisp blue sky. You have to work at being bored in these surroundings.

Paddling back to the town landing, wishing after all that I had brought along a rod and tried for lunch, I was mentally listing the images that I would take away from this venture in history: the perfect reflection of Hamburg Bridge on the surface of the river when all conditions of sky and water are right...a birchbark canoe with one Indian holding a spear, the other a torch that lighted the walls of the primeval forest...the builder of the first scow at Reed's Landing standing in its stern and pushing off...100 oxen dragging heavy carts to Hamburg's wharves...a schooner under sail in the Upper Bay...millions of tiny shad splashing down the Connecticut in September to begin their miraculous migration...the elm tree on Timothy Tiffany's land...what rum and burned sugar must have tasted like on a frigid stone pier...the six inches of snow in a trembling shad boat...the black river world when there was no moon...casting from our hangar deck with rod in one hand, our newest son in my other...the smell of white perch chowder...the moment when Huey and LaPlace realized they had a nine-foot sturgeon in their net...the sign in the Old Lyme Sea Food Market each April announcing "Fresh Connecticut River Shad"...the shad boats (one-lungers) puffing out of Hamburg Cove at dusk...and the sweet tug of a largemouth bass racing for a sunken tree in the Eight Mile River.

∾

CARLIN KINDILIEN *has lived in Lyme since 1957 and in one of Hamburg Cove's best-known houses for part of that time. He is the author of five nonfiction books and writes frequently for popular magazines. He spends a good part of every summer introducing his grandchildren to the joys of bass fishing in the Eight Mile River.*

∼ VI ∼

STERLING CITY AND HAMBURG

by ELIZEBETH B. PLIMPTON

T oday, Hamburg Road (Connecticut Route 156) runs more or less straight north from the top of Lord Hill and crosses Falls Brook (sometimes called Falls River by old-timers) at a point where it forms a sizable deadwater that rises and falls with the tide in Hamburg Cove. But before 1810, as the road descended the lower reaches of the hill, it bent sharply to the east; crossed Falls Brook at its narrowest point just below a natural dam of solid rock and above the falls that gave the stream its name; and then a short distance beyond the bridge, doubled back westward until it bent once more to the north and eventually rejoined Hamburg Road. The winding road, shaped like the uprights of an intoxicated A—and with a short crosspiece between the uprights—was and is Sterling City Road, so called because it passed through Sterling City, a tiny community settled by the Sterling family in the 1700s.

I know the area well. My great-grandfather and grandfather and mother lived there, and although I was born in Hartford, I spent vacations and every Sunday afternoon here as a child and

The Mill Pond on Falls Brook. From here the brook flows over a dam and under Sterling City Road, then plunges past the old grist mill and sawmill into the broad valley leading to Hamburg Cove.

became a resident in the '30s. I have seen many changes. In the '30s, Sterling City was a community of worn-out and crumbling houses populated by longtime residents with enormous families and little else. The Depression hit the people very hard—the same as it did almost everyone in southeastern Connecticut—but they survived somehow. Those who are alive today are fine, upstanding people, but they're not living in Sterling City. Along in the '60s and early '70s, they began selling out to the new people who were moving into Lyme from Fairfield County and New York. The old, tired houses have been rebuilt and enlarged, and new ones have been added. Sterling City is alive again, but not in the way it was two or three hundred years ago.

It's said that Sterling City Road was once an Indian trail. Today, though black-topped, it still has aspects of a trail. It's a pleasure to walk, as long as you stick close to the road edges and keep an eye and ear out for cars coming too fast. Moving at an easy, steady pace, you can go from one end of the road to the other in a half hour or less. Let's do it now, starting at the southern end.

Here is beautiful Tiffany Farm, one of only two dairy farms left in Lyme, the mecca for practically every modern-day artist and photographer. Captain Samuel Selden started the farm in 1741 when he bought nineteen acres in the Sterling City area from Jonathan Reed and built the substantial two-story house soon after.[1]

In the *Selden Ancestry*, the authors write: "There is a tradition in the Selden Family that the fair Deborah . . . had another suitor, whom she jilted for Samuel Selden . . . Captain Samuel Selden, who had been absent on some military duty, on his return, passing through Chester, observed a notice on the door of their then meeting house that 'Noadiah Brainard and Deborah Dudley propose marriage in this house on the next Lord's Day.' He tore the notice from the door, replacing it with another, substituting his name for that of the unfortunate swain. 'Samuel Selden of Lyme and Deborah Dudley of Saybrook, intend marriage in this house next Lord's Day.' When the day arrived, Captain Selden arrived early on the steps of the meeting house, armed and equipped according to law. Seeing that his notice was undisturbed, he waited. In due time the congregation began to enter the meeting house, likewise the minister, all of them observing the notice. Shortly Lieutenant Joseph Dudley, his wife, and daughter approached. Samuel Selden spoke a few words to Deborah, greeted her affectionately, took her arm, walked in, and up the aisle, and they were married according to the solemn forms then obtaining. In true Lochinvar fashion, he carried off his bride across the river to 'Twelve Mile Island Farm.' Not a word of objection or sign of resistance was made at that time nor later."

After Samuel's death, his widow married her faithful Noadiah

Brainard. He died within the year, and she lived out her life with her son, Ezra, who had inherited the farm on Sterling City Road. Charles E. Tiffany bought the farm in 1841, and it has remained in his family ever since. And now that Jack Tiffany has sold the development rights to the farm to the state under the state's farm-land preservation law, the land will remain open—can never be developed—in perpetuity.

Not far beyond Tiffany Farm, Sterling City Road splits. Birch Mill Road, once called Lower Sterling City Road, dips down on the left. Sterling City Road proper continues straight ahead to the small bridge spanning Falls Brook. The stream has its source at Norwich Pond way back in the forest. It flows into Uncas Lake, formerly known as Hog Pond, and on through scrubby, swampy forest until it reaches Mill Pond, which lies quiet above the steep natural falls that tumble into the mill race. From there, it wanders on through the valley until it joins Hamburg Cove.

Mill Pond today is partially silted in and inhabited by ducks and geese, but when I was growing up, it was wonderful for ice skating. We'd get on it at the bridge and skate all the way up to the Crossway —where the present road into the Nehantic State Forest crosses the brook—and sometimes we could go all the way to Pine Island between the Crossway and the dam at Uncas Lake. You can't do that today, of course, because the open fields of the past have now been taken over by woods, and the area right along Falls Brook is a dense alder swamp.

In 1709, Captain Daniel Sterling, the progenitor of the Ster-lings of Lyme, bought an interest in the water power generated by Falls Brook, and he soon purchased a number of properties in the area. The house on the left just beyond the falls was built by him. Years later, it was occupied for half a century by the Edward B. Otis family. Ed Otis lived to be 101, and I remember him clearly. He worked here and there as a hired hand on the farms. He used to split wood for my uncle. As was the custom in those days when dinnertime came at noon, hired hands and employers sat down at the table together. I recall Mr. Otis's one day eating a whole bowlful of stewed tomatoes that were meant for everybody. It didn't bother him a bit. He was a kind of character—as many Sterling City people were. After his wife died, he remarked that he hadn't known he was "going to miss the old woman so much."

Just beyond the Daniel Sterling-Otis house, on the south side of the road, is the large center-chimney house built by William Ely in the late 1600s.[2] This eventually became a Sterling property, and after Daniel acquired Biggs Meadow between the house and brook, the Sterlings established their family cemetery. A high stone wall now hides the ancient gravestones from the road.

The Ely house belonged to my great-grandfather, Noah Harding, and grandfather, Lyman Harding, for many years. My grandfather built a long, narrow porch or gallery of rather modest Victorian design across the front and lengthened the windows down to the floor. A subsequent owner removed the porch, changed the windows again, and rebuilt the front entrance. It had originally been a simple Colonial doorway; today, it's a fine square-topped entrance of Georgian design. Grandpa Harding always wanted everything new that came along, so he put in modern plumbing, but he still kept the many-holed privy that had bright blue, plastered inside walls. The thing I liked the best about

The William Ely house overlooking the Mill Pond was built soon after the turn of the seventeenth century. It has had several owners and has been remodeled frequently and rather extensively.

the place was the land around it. It was all open. The hill directly behind the house was covered with birdfoot violets.

The next old house after the Ely house belonged to Josiah Hawes, the first minister to serve the church in its present home (1814–1833). Two great spiritual revivals took place in his nineteen years in Lyme.[3]

Beyond the Hawes house, Sterling City Road makes a sharp turn to the left. The road straight ahead is Sterling Hill Road. Let's take it easy here. The road is steep, and you'll stretch your muscles and perhaps stop to catch your breath before you reach the Stephen Sterling house. You won't regret the effort. It's a charming house built in 1740 by John Sterling. It's a little crooked and very weatherbeaten, but it is country New England from sill to chimney top. Until 1950, it was owned by direct descendants of John—all named Sterling. Its present owner is an indirect descendant of the Sterlings.

Returning to Sterling City Road, we continue westward on its northern leg. Almost immediately, we come to a tiny rushing brook that flows under the road and down into the valley to join Falls Brook. This is Fulling Mill Brook. It played an important role in the economy of the early settlement, because a fulling mill was established on its bank. The mill had several functions. First, it scoured the lanolin from the cloth that the women wove from yarn derived from area sheep. Then, the cloth was thickened and tightened by revolving drums of teasel pods, which also raised the nap. Finally, the cloth was dyed.

A short distance down the brook, below Sterling City Road, was a tannery, another Sterling family business. Here the raw hides taken from farm animals became leather for boots and shoes.[4]

A little west of the brook, Birch Mill Road—which is the cross-arm of the A formed by this somewhat confusing road network—bumps into Sterling City Road. On the southwest corner of the intersection stood the home of the Reverend David Huntington, who was called to the church in Lyme in 1802. He served nine years and died suddenly after preaching two sermons the previous day. The second sermon took as its text, "Set thine house in order for thou shall die and not live." His gravestone in the North Lyme Cemetery records this incident. Mr. Huntington is also remembered for the fire-and-brimstone sermons he preached. The Nehantic Indians, it is said, especially liked the summer camp meetings on Brown Hill, when he expounded on the road to hell that "is paved with the skulls of unbaptized babies."[5]

Turning to the left onto Birch Mill Road, we descend a short, steep grade to a saltbox house that was probably built by William Sill. In 1789 he married Jemima Sterling, the daughter of Captain William Sterling. It was in this house that a tragedy occurred. The *Connecticut Gazette* of July 24, 1805, reported it this way:

"On Monday last, was committed to prison in this city [New London], William Sill for the murder of his father-in-law, Captain William Sterling. Mr. Sill has for a number of years been troubled with the hypochondria and in consequence, has had frequent recourse to opium and occasionally to ardent spirits.

"From the too frequent use of these, he had been subject to delirious turns which generally lasted three or four days. One of these fits attacked him on Saturday last and his wife, as she had before done, fled for safety with her children, to her father's house. Early on Monday morning, Captain Sterling, partly for the purpose of getting some clothes for the children and for finding the situation of his son-in-law, went to the house, accompanied by his son and a neighbor. They found Mr. Sill apparently rational and in unusual good spirits. Captain Sterling took a seat directly facing a bedroom door and Sill soon after went into the bedroom but immediately returned with a loaded gun in his hands, which he instantly discharged at Captain Sterling. The contents lodged in his bosom. Sill then aimed a blow with the breach of his gun at the son of Captain Sterling, but fortunately his arm received it. Sill was then secured..."[6]

Sill was tried for murder at Norwich and, in spite of his undoubted guilt, was acquitted on his plea of insanity.[6] He lived in Old Saybrook until his death.

The Stephen Sterling house on Sterling Hill Road was built in 1740. One of its most recent owners was Mary Sterling Bakke, author of A Sampler of Lifestyles - Womanhood and Youth in Colonial Lyme.

Following the Sills, Elisha Miller made and sold shoes in the old saltbox. In more recent years, the house was occupied by the family of James Miller, who was a descendant of Elisha and a night watchman for the Dickinson Witch Hazel Company in Essex. He sometimes commuted from home to Essex by bicycle, but more often he rode to Ely's Ferry, put his bicycle into a boat, and rowed across the river.

Beyond the Sill-Miller house, Birch Mill Road crosses the valley floor to a bridge over Falls Brook. To the right of the bridge is the valley shaped by the brook on its way to Hamburg Cove. In the immediate foreground is a deadwater created only about ten years ago by the nearby landowner. Beyond it, the stream snakes through a marsh and grows gradually wider until it almost—but not quite—deserves to be called a river.

The land just to the left of the bridge is low and frequently flooded by beavers, whose lodge you can see. From there it slopes

In the 1789 saltbox on Birch Mill Road, William Sill, who probably built the house, murdered his father-in-law, Captain William Sterling.

upward gently, then makes a prodigious leap almost straight up to Sterling City Road. After a storm, you can hear the roar of falling water. This is the site of the ancient gristmill built by Captain Daniel Sterling. Located at the foot of the precipitous, narrow falls, the mill for many years ground the grain grown on nearby farms. The miller poured the grain into a hopper, from which it trickled down through the eye of the upper millstone onto a bedstone. As the upper stone turned over the bedstone, it scraped off husks and pulverized the grain into a smooth, fine sand that passed through grooves in the stone onto a revolving sieve. All this was powered by the overshot water wheel.

Eventually, with the development of mechanical power and the production of huge amounts of western grain, the gristmill stopped operating. A shoddy picker was then attached to the mill wheel. Shoddy was made of old rags that were pulled apart and shredded. It was sold to Danbury hatters for felt hats and could also be spun into coarse yarn and woven into everyday clothing. Unhappily, it was also flammable. One day the shoddy picker struck a spark. The nearby shoddy caught fire, and the old mill was destroyed. Today a house stands on its foundations.

There used to be a sawmill below the gristmill. It too was powered by Falls Brook and had an overshot waterwheel like that of the grist mill. Around the middle of the nineteenth century, both mills were sold, and in the early 1900s, the sawmill was used for chipping witch hazel and birch brush. The operation was owned by the E. E. Dickinson Company of Essex. Local land-owners cut the brush and took it to the mill where it was weighed and then chopped by water power-driven machinery before it was transported to Essex for distillation.

(Probably the first birch mill operating in Lyme was near the north end of Sterling City Road opposite the Irvine House.)

If we continue westward on Birch Mill Road from Falls Brook, we shall pass a couple of small, old houses that were proba-bly built for the mill workers. But let's retrace our steps to the road's eastern intersection with Sterling City Road. Here, opposite the Huntington House, stood a red house belonging to Alfred Lester. Because it was on the direct route, as then traveled, from Ely's Ferry to Meeting House Hill and then to Reed's Landing or to the trail leading to East Haddam, the house was a tavern or per-haps a halfway house in early days. A large room on the second floor had a folding partition that could be closed to divide the room into two small spaces or opened to be used for community gatherings and dances.

Opposite Alfred Lester's house was the home of his father, James. When the latter died in 1891, he was only a few months short of 100.

In very early years, sixteen houses were clustered in this area, and all were occupied by Sterlings. A blacksmith's shop, cobbler's shop, clothier's store, general store, and cider mill were included in the group. This was the heart of Sterling City. It was just a collec-tion of houses. People sometimes ask me, "Where was Sterling City? Why was it called a city?" This is where it was. It was called a city because it was a center of industry.

Sterling City, a cluster of houses, as painted by Winfield Scott Clime (1881-1958) in the early 1900s. Unfinished oil on canvas. COLLECTION OF ELIZEBETH B. PLIMPTON.

Sterling City Road rises at this point, and as it levels off, there on the hilltop to the north stands the home of the unfortunate Captain William Sterling. He built it about 1763 for his bride, Jemima Sill Sterling.

Next we come to a house that incorporates the original building of the Sterling City School, School District No. 6. The school was closed in 1935, but the initials of early students are still visible on its walls. The first person to arrive at school in the morning had to light the wood stove. A pail of drinking water was brought from the well of the house next door. Two outhouses substituted for modern plumbing. The turnover of young, inexperienced female teachers was considerable in winter when older, bigger, rambunctious boys attended, so the school was often taught by a man during that period.

Next to the school stood the home of Edward Volkert, an artist best known for his paintings of the oxen that used to be so prevalent in the area. For his living room walls, he painted panels that could be reversed to show the current season. The house was demolished in 1990, but Volkert's studio remains.

A little farther along, Stone Post Road drops down the hill to the left. This is a modern road leading to a modern subdivision of beautiful antique houses that were doomed for extinction by distant municipalities until the developers came along, dismantled them piece by piece, and then reconstructed them in Falls Brook Valley.

About a tenth of a mile west of Stone Post Road, a grassy lane know as Meeting House Hill Road branches to the right from Sterling City Road and runs behind the home of Wilson Irvine, another Lyme artist. The main part of the house, which now belongs to Irvine descendants, was built in 1842 by the Reverend Charles W. Murdock. He died two years later before it was completed.[8]

In 1724, the lane was the last link in the highway that began at what is now Tiffany Farm and looped around Falls Brook Valley. From its start at Sterling City Road, Meeting House Hill Road cut across country to a point just above where Joshuatown Road meets Hamburg Road, then continued on to Old Hamburg, or Reed's Landing, where the Old Hamburg Bridge crosses the Eight Mile River. According to the custom of the day, the first meeting house was built on the highest point along the road. Nothing remains of the building, but it is thought to have been a simple frame structure measuring about twenty by thirty feet,

The main part of the Wilson Irvine house was built in 1842. Meeting House Hill Road, now nothing more than a grassy lane, ran behind it, connecting Sterling City Road to Hamburg Road and the Old Hamburg Bridge.

without porch, chimney, or steeple. The building was probably not completed until about 1728.

In 1810, the present highway (Route 156) was laid out. It ran from Tiffany's corner into Hamburg Village. Sterling City Road was extended to meet it at what is now the Grange Hall, and eventually, Meeting House Hill Road fell into disuse (but it remains a trail that I still love to walk). A major change in the community followed quickly.

Prior to that time, the village of Hamburg was nothing. There were no buildings, just a few docks. The place was known as Harvey's Plains. The "Harvey" came without doubt from the Harvey family. The "Plains" cannot be accounted for. Hamburg is certainly not built on a plain, but in the very early 1800s, Harvey's Plains must have offered certain attractions—especially the Cove and its waterfront. So when the new road came through, there was a shift of population from Sterling City and other parts of Lyme toward the water.

The population move did not, however, bring with it a change in the name of the hamlet that sprang up. As nearly as anyone can determine, Harvey's Plains did not become Hamburg until some time before June 17, 1828, when Ezra Pratt, the first postmaster of the first post office in the village, postmarked letters "Hamburgh." No one is certain why the change occurred. Frances Arnold Lagel has the best explanation. She told me: "The story I got from Reginald Lord, who learned it from his father, starts with some sailors rowing in from the outer cove where their ship was at anchor. They were struck by the similarity between the Eight Mile River and the Elbe River in their native Hamburg, Germany. They tied up at the landing and went to the general store. There, sitting around the cracker barrel and a barrel of rum, they talked with the local people about the two rivers and joked that our village should be called Hamburg. The name stuck.

"During the Tall Ship celebration in 1976, a family from Hamburg, Germany, tied up at Cove Landing. I talked with them, and they agreed with the early sailors that our Eight Mile River is very much like their River Elbe." So much for how Harvey's Plains became Hamburg.

One of the first things to be built in the new community—as in most God-fearing Yankee towns—was the church. That was in 1814. If it's true, as has been said, that a few timbers from the earlier church on Meeting House Hill Road are incorporated in the attic of the Hamburg Church, that must mean that the old church was razed as the new one was erected. Be that as it may, the new church was bigger and better in every way, and standing on a hilltop as it does, it commands a view of the hills that dramatically ring the Upper Bay of Hamburg Cove and, in turn, can be seen from almost every point on those hills.

The Hamburg Church (properly known as the First Congregational Church of Lyme) is not so celebrated for its beauty as

The First Congregational Church of Lyme sits high on a hill in Hamburg over-looking Hamburg Cove's Upper Bay. This is the church's second home; its first building was on Meeting House Hill Road. Copper engraving by Thomas Nason (1888-1971) in the Lyme Town Hall.

many New England churches, but it's typical of the lower Connecticut River Valley in its substantial charm and the simplicity of the four-column portico. At first, the church auditorium was on the ground floor and a gallery bordered it on both sides and above the vestibule. But in 1948, in order to pay for repairs to the building, the church fathers gave the town certain privileges "to have and to hold" as long as the building stood. That was when the church was remodeled to put the auditorium on the second floor and the town meeting room on the first. The church today retains this plan, although the contract with the town has been nullified, and the first floor is used for Sunday School classes and church functions. The Lyme Library was also housed here until 1969. A wing was recently added to the building to house church offices; the kitchen, a downstairs meeting room, and an inclinator to help the handicapped get to the church auditorium.

Behind the church is the North Lyme Cemetery. Established in 1854, it was the first cemetery in North Lyme (now Lyme) where a man might buy a burial plot and have it exclusively for his own. Prior to that time, burials were made in various places, and no attention was paid to ownership, maintenance, or even preservation.[9]

The Lyme Grange Hall is across Sterling City Road from the church at the intersection of Sterling City and Hamburg Roads. Behind the hall are the Hamburg Fair Grounds. When the Grange was formed in 1896, it rented the lower floor of what is now a house between Hamburg and Old Hamburg Roads. The second floor was occupied by the Pythagoras Lodge of Masons, which owned the building. The first Hamburg Fair was held there on September 30, 1897. This was such a success that the Grange bought its present building, an old store falling into ruin. With volunteer help, the place was renovated, and the three acres behind it cleared. The second fair was held there the following year. The fair has been held every year since except for two years during World War II.[10]

Today's two-and-a-half-day fairs still have horse and cattle pulls and vegetable and fruit competitions, but these events are rather incidental to the mechanical rides and similar entertainments that are brought in by outsiders. In the old days when the fair lasted only one day and was held on Wednesdays and the children had the day off from school, agriculture ruled the roost. A full-fledged horse show was held, and the competition between the yokes of oxen was a great spectacle. Long trains of oxen were brought in by their owners from all around the state. In his memoirs, Joshua Warren Stark, who was first selectman of the Town of Lyme for twenty-six years, noted that one year more than 200 yokes of oxen were on hand.

Until the twentieth century, oxen and horses were essential in

Scores, even hundreds, of oxen used to be brought to the Hamburg Fair where they vied in pulling competitions and were sold. POSTCARD, COLLECTION OF MICHAEL LLOYD.

Lyme. So it is not surprising that in 1858, Ephraim Otis Reynolds set up a carriage and wagon manufacturing shop in a three-story building on Hamburg Road across from the church and just north of the present H. L. Reynolds Co. store. Behind the shop, which once employed six to eight men, a blacksmith shop was located in the north end of what is now the residence of Leland H. Reynolds. Nearby on the shore of the Cove stood an ice house. Ephraim Reynolds also opened and ran the general store that is operated today by his great-granddaughter, Jane Reynolds Rowland DeWolf. Before 1962, the post office was in that store.

In an article printed in *Tidings* in 1989, Mrs. DeWolf wrote about the store as described by her mother, Harriet Reynolds Rowland, who was also postmistress for thirty-five years. "…long counters, one on each side. Food on one side, miscellaneous things, cloths by the yard, men's coats, pants, shoes, boots, ladies' clothes; you asked for it, we had it, corsets, stockings, and ribbons. In the center of the room was a pot belly stove; a spittoon was placed nearby for customers who chewed tobacco. The grocery department had everything you could think of. All the goodies came in large boxes, tubs and barrels; they had to be opened and dealt out by the pound or quart. You had to weigh everything ...Sugar, molasses, crackers came in barrels; cheese, 20 to 25 pounds of salt pork...The candy counter...long trays of chocolate drops, peppermints...stick candy for a penny. The back room was called the grain room; there was row after row of grain, oats, corn...kegs of nails...In the attic, things not too often called for were kept, like lamps and lamp chimneys, bolts, nuts, screws, and thread for sewing in many colors. The merchant did the work; customers didn't push a cart and come to you to check out."

Mrs. DeWolf adds: "I still run the store very much as my father and grandfather did...Items are left at the store for someone else to pick up. I have a collection of works by local artists, post-cards, antiques—and memories from the good old days when times were slower and more rewarding. My daughters join me now on weekends, and thus the H. L. Reynolds Co. general store continues into the fifth generation."

At one time, the Reynolds store was just one of four in Ham-burg. One of the others was owned by Mosely Brockway. It is, perhaps, remembered best for a slight mix-up Brockway had with Hazard Wilcox, who was noted for his wit and ability to avoid paying bills. One day Brockway asked Hazard to come to the store to look over his account, which was in arrears. They went through the account book noting that on a certain date, Wilcox had bought something for so much; and on another date, ditto, so much; and on another date, ditto, so much. Finally Wilcox inter-rupted the reading. "Hold on there," he exclaimed. "That's a mistake. We haven't had any ditto in the house this year." To which, Brockway replied: "You go home and ask your wife what ditto means, and when you come down again, drop in and we will

The H. L. Reynolds Co. store on Hamburg Road in the center of Hamburg. Opened in 1859, it is still going strong. There were once three other stores in Hamburg.

see if we can get somewhere." It was some time before Wilcox reappeared. "You found out what ditto means?" Brockway asked. "I've found out that I'm a damn fool and you're ditto," Wilcox answered.[11]

In the early 1900s, as the newfangled automobile began to catch on, the Reynolds carriage shop was forced out of business. (The building was eventually sold and moved to become the center section of the large house north of the present auto salesroom.) It was succeeded in time by an automobile repair shop run by Donald G. Reynolds that was a little south of and behind the general store. By 1924, the new shop had outgrown its quarters, and a new building—the present garage—was started. It was an unusual structure for a New England village because it was built of stone.

This came about because, shortly after the Civil War, a Lyme resident proposed to pay all costs of erecting an elaborate stone church if the town's people would provide the stone. The proposal was accepted, and work began in 1873. Then, the donor ran into financial trouble and withdrew his offer.[12] For years the unfinished walls stood in mute hope that the church might someday be finished, but nothing happened until finally Donald Reynolds bought some of the stone for his garage.

The garage is now run by a third generation of Reynolds—Gary. On the Cove back of the building stands the Reynolds Marina, established by Donald in 1939.

Across Hamburg Road and a few doors down from the store is the Lyme Public Hall, dedicated in 1887. This came into being when a group of citizens felt a need for a place for community social events. All went well with the undertaking until it came time to select a site for the hall, then tempers flared, and a power struggle ensued. Captain James Bill paid $200 for the land on which the hall stands and offered it to the association for $20. Since there was no restriction on membership, anyone who paid the twenty-five cents dues could vote; so members were brought in from Essex and Old Lyme. Jefferson Bill, then living in New York, traveled out with a number of new voters. Captain Bill's wife, who hadn't been away from home in twenty-five years, came to vote. Captain Bill won, but the feeling of the opposition was bitter, and they immediately withdrew and formed an association of their own. Despite this, the new Public Hall was a success and became the center of the town's social life. Dances were held on Thanksgiving and Christmas as well as on other occasions.[15]

In 1952 the town, needing a place to keep its fire equipment, leased the building for fifteen years and built Lyme's first firehouse in a new excavation beneath the structure. Six years later, with mortgage payments to be met, the association was dissolved, and the building was turned over to the town in payment of the debt. The building continued to serve as headquarters of the Lyme Volunteer Fire Company and as the setting for its annual public

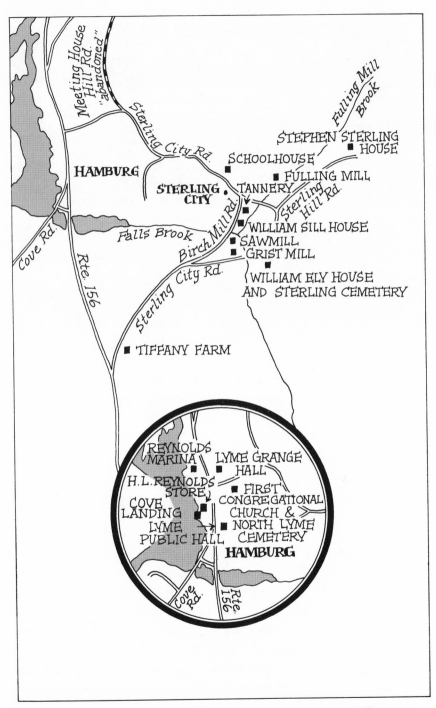

Before 1810, Hamburg Road (Route 156) stopped at what is now Tiffany Farm, and those traveling north followed Sterling City Road around to Meeting House Hill Road, which rejoined Hamburg Road.

Reynolds Boat Yard *painted by Albertus Jones (1882-1957), is now known as the Reynolds Marina, on Hamburg Cove's Upper Bay. Jones and his wife spent their summers on the black boat at the end of the dock. Watercolor.* COLLECTION OF MRS. CARROLL DUNHAM.

dinner until 1985 when a new public safety complex was constructed south of Falls Brook, and the old building then fell into disuse. It was not, however, abandoned. A new Lyme Public Hall Association was formed, and the town gave it a fifty-five-year lease on the building. The building has now been completely renovated, and once again it is used for lectures, receptions, dinners, etc.

Opposite the Public Hall is an erstwhile store building. Tradition has it that the first building on the site was a trading post. The James L. Lord family owned the entire property from Hamburg Cove to Hamburg Road. They operated Lord's Store, a general merchandise business, as well as a dock. The dock was an especially busy place after 1887 when a new organization named the

Hamburg Cove, 1906 *was painted by Richard L. Brooks from a photograph and is a faithful portrait of Hamburg almost a century ago. The ship in the foreground, the Tansy Bitters, is being poled through the narrow channel by two men, one on each side of the deck. Oil on canvas.* COLLECTIONS OF CONNECTICUT RIVER MUSEUM, ESSEX, CONN.

Eight Mile River Channel Company widened and deepened the channel through the Cove.[14]

For many years after that, Lyme enjoyed a flourishing lumber trade, with coasters picking up lumber and railroad ties from all the docks on a regular basis. As many as one hundred vessels a year went out loaded with wood products and returned with supplies for the Lyme stores.[15] Some shad fishermen also kept their boats at the docks and unloaded their catches and dried their nets there while others had their own fish places around the Cove. During shad season in early spring, we could buy a whole fresh fish at the dock for a quarter.

Eventually in 1943, the Lords sold their property to the DeSaulnier and Lagel families, who renamed it Cove Landing. The Lagels ran the Cove Landing Boatyard and Marina, which are now operated by John Leonard. The DeSaulniers ran Cove Landing Store and did a thriving business in gourmet foods. Rudy Mertz presided over the meat department and was famed for his prime cuts.

The Cove Landing Store had several owners after the DeSaulniers gave up the business, but, it was a downhill struggle for them. Competition from the Old Lyme and Old Saybrook supermarkets was too much, and finally the little store was shuttered.

Over the years, a similar fate has befallen most attempts at commercial enterprise in Hamburg and Sterling City. Yet the area that comprises both communities is very alive today. Somehow it has learned to live with and enjoy change. It still retains the serene, unhurried vitality that seems to have characterized it one, two, and three centuries ago.

∾

ELIZEBETH B. PLIMPTON *is municipal historian of the Town of Lyme. She was co-author of* The Lieutenant River, *published by the Lyme Historical Society/Florence Griswold Museum in 1991. Her maternal great-grandfather was a resident of Sterling City, and she herself came to live on Sterling City Road in 1938.*

~ VII ~

THE ELYS AND ELY TAVERN

by CHAMBERLAIN FERRY

The Sterlings and the Elys, along with the Lords, were the leading families of the Hamburg Cove neighborhood in its early days. The Sterlings owned numerous bits and pieces of land east of the Cove. The Elys owned one huge piece of land directly south of the Cove. The Sterlings were industrialists; the Elys, basically, farmers, although they were also engaged in several other businesses. Both families intermarried extensively with other area families, but if a census were taken, it would in all likelihood show that there are today more Ely descendants than Sterling. Of the several possible reasons for this, one is that the Elys came first.

Richard Ely I arrived in Lyme just about the time the town was split off from Saybrook in 1665. Born in England in about 1620, Richard became a shipping merchant in Plymouth, then emigrated to Boston in America about forty-one years later. There he took his third wife—a widow, Elizabeth Fenwick Cullick. She had inherited from her brother, Colonel George Fenwick, of Saybrook, about one hundred acres on the Lyme mainland and the

Richard Ely II built the small center section of this house for his son Samuel, c. 1700. The beautiful two-and-a-half story Georgian front section was added a half century later.

Six Mile Island (now Nott's Island) farm. Unfortunately, Mrs. Cullick's property was in debt, and Richard had to pay this off before he could take the land over. To accomplish this, he took up residence in Lyme.

At the time that Richard was getting established with a new wife in a new part of the world, his son William, who had been born in England in 1647, was living in the West Indies with an uncle. Now he sailed to Lyme to join his father and a half-brother, Richard II, who was ten years his junior. This was in about 1668; Richard II had preceded him by two years.

All three Elys became large landowners. Richard I set the pace when he asked the General Court to grant him additional upland to supplement the farm on Nott's Island. According to the town records for 1676, the court came through in handsome fashion, granting Richard enough land to bring his total holding to more than 3,000 acres. The property was bounded on the north by Hamburg Cove (then designated as the Eight Mile River), on the west by the Connecticut River, on the east by a "grindell running out of a rock at the point of Peck's" (a spring probably now hidden under the pond north of Tinker Lane and Ely's Ferry Road), and on the south by the Monechoge River (Lord's Creek and Lord's Cove). This land had formerly incorporated a sizable Indian settlement. Richard Ely's sons, William and Richard II, later added 1,300 acres to the estate.

That Richard I was a man of importance is indicated by the magnitude of this grant, but we don't know much about him otherwise. William was also a man of importance. He repeatedly served the town in the offices of lister, townsman, selectman, fence viewer, surveyor, and moderator. He also served on many committees conducting various kinds of town business, and he represented Lyme at the courts in Hartford, New London, and New Haven. From 1689 to 1706 he was Lyme's deputy to the General Court. In 1708 he was admitted to the bar. In 1697 he was appointed captain of the Train band, a military group, and took part in an expedition against Port Royal and Nova Scotia.[1]

The location of Richard I's home is unknown. Richard II built his house in 1684 on the north side of Ely's Ferry Road, now three houses in from Hamburg Road.[2] It was extensively remodeled a little more than 300 years after its construction. It is not only the oldest Ely house still standing, but it is also one of the oldest in the Connecticut River Valley.

William Ely built what was known as his "mansion" on the north side of Ely's Ferry Road at the extreme western end, within a couple hundred feet of the Connecticut River. There is no record of the exact date when construction was started, but it was probably in the 1680s. The house continued growing over the years until it was an edifice of twenty-four rooms. This would seem to put it more in a class with the early great houses along Virginia's James River than with anything of the same period in New England. But that is strictly conjectural. The early history of the house is limited to two memories: Many years ago an Ely born in the house was told by his mother that the house faced south and had a central hall, indicating that it was probably of the Geor-

Built about 1684, the Richard Ely II house is the oldest in the Hamburg Cove area. Print from The Ely Ancestry, *published in 1902. The house was considerably remodeled in 1990.*

gian style. The Morgan sisters, who lived in the third dwelling to the east, believed that the house had silver doorknobs.

William Ely died in 1717, and his descendants occupied the house through the 1700s and pretty well into the nineteenth century. Family records note that, during the occupancy of a Charles Ely, Daniel Webster once appeared at the Ely landing with the request that he be taken across the Connecticut River.[3] But the river was crowded with broken ice and a crossing was impossible. So Webster spent the night at the Elys' and was entertained at the card table.

The Connecticut River is narrower at the place where William Ely built his mansion than for some distance upstream and down, and in early years it was often suggested that a public ferry be authorized there.

Finally in 1800, in response to a 1760 petition from an Ely, the state's governor and council directed that a ferry be "set up and kept." The ferry would be known as Cullick Ely's Ferry, and the rates it could charge would be:

> Man, Horse and Load - 12 cts 5 mils
>
> Footman - 4 cts 2 mils
>
> Led Horse - 10 cts
>
> Ox or other Neat Kine - 12 cts 5 mils
>
> Swine, Sheep or Goats - 1 ct 4 mils

"and the fare for every two wheeled carriage, with one man and draught horse, shall be double; and for every four wheeled carriage, one man and draught horse, treble the fare for a man, horse and load, as above stated; and for every additional Person, or horse or other Beast, the same as above stated."[4]

Similar rate schedules were approved for the Brockway's, Warner's, Chapman's, Easthampton, and Middletown ferries. But the Ely's Ferry rates were about fifty percent higher than the others.

The vessels used were flat-bottomed scows propelled by sweeps or sails. During the later years of the ferry, which was operated by Fred Wilkie until about 1935, a gasoline-powered launch moved the scow. There are various pictures of the ferry. The only one dated is an 1879 oil painting by Carleton Wiggins; it shows a scow without mast or sail carrying a hay wagon. One photograph from the Wilkie family photos shows what appears to be the Wiggins ferry at anchor off Ely's Landing. Another, owned by the Connecticut River Museum, features a similar craft but with leeboards, an off-center mast, and articulated bow and stern ramps. By contrast, the ferry pictured by Wiggins had fixed bow and stern extensions that slanted out and slightly upward.[5]

The landings on both sides of the river consisted of stone ramps slanting from the banks and of such height and length as to give the ferryboat a solid surface on which to beach and take on or

Ely's Ferry painted in 1879 by Carleton Wiggins was a flat-bottomed scow propelled by sweeps or sails. The artist should not be confused with his son, Guy Carleton Wiggins, who did paintings of Hamburg Cove. Oil on canvas. PRIVATE COLLECTION.

disembark vehicles at any stage of the tide. These structures, somewhat scattered, are still visible; the one on the east side is an extension of Ely's Ferry Road. From the stone ramp on the Essex side, a road ran south alongside the river to Essex Island, where a drawbridge crossed to Ferry Road. In 1822 this part of the route was incorporated as the Essex Turnpike and was part of an alternate Boston Post Road.[6] (With the help of a ferry authorized in 1667, the original Post Road crossed from Saybrook to Old Lyme.) In 1824, by the addition of a new Salem-Hamburg Turnpike, the alternate Post Road rejoined the original Post Road well east of Old Lyme. Thus people living near the mouth of the Connecticut River had one more way to cross the river than they do today.

The establishment of Cullick Ely's Ferry seems to have encouraged the construction of several new buildings in the general neighborhood of the William Ely mansion. What is now a handsome Greek Revival home facing the river and just south of Ely's Ferry Road once housed the ferry operator. There was another residence a few hundred yards to the south, but in the 1930s it was put aboard a scow and moved to Old Lyme.[7] For many years, S.C. Ely had a store near the ferry operator's home. Photographs in the Wilkie collection show it in two locations, but it left no foundations. Surprisingly, there is no evidence that any of the buildings in this cluster had wells. Perhaps the river water was not too salty to drink—particularly on a falling tide. And of course there was no pollution.

Less than a mile east of the river, Richard Ely II built houses for his sons Samuel and Richard III. Both houses still stand on the north side of Ely's Ferry Road. Samuel's house is now surrounded by great trees, including an enormous white oak. It is one of New England's loveliest small Georgian dwellings, with a handsome doorway and Palladian window. It is presently owned and occupied by Richard F. Cooper, Jr., the grandson of the Cooper who in 1925 purchased the Clews estate consisting of former Ely acreage with over a mile of river and cove frontage. Richard Ely III's house is one door farther east, a much simpler house but one favored by Indians who, with the owner's permission, would slip through the back door on cold nights and sleep on the keeping room floor. In the morning, before the owners awoke, they would disappear, leaving the fire blazing in the fireplace.[8]

Further change came to the Ely's Landing neighborhood when steam came to the Connecticut River. Before that, because sailing ships were so dependent on wind, current, and tide, river traffic could not be precisely scheduled. Steam corrected that.

In 1813 the *Julianna* ran between Hartford and Middletown on a three- or four-hour schedule, but the service was not continued long. In 1815 the *Fulton*, which regularly connected New Haven and New York, made a side trip to Hartford. Her owners somehow persuaded the authorities to give them a monopoly on traffic into and out of New York.[9] [10] As a result, in 1822, when the

This Victorian house on the banks of the Connecticut River just south of Ely's Ferry was owned by Frederick Wilkie, last operator of Ely's Ferry. Some time after 1935, the property was bought by Elisha Cooper, and it was later remodeled along Greek Revival lines by his son Richard. The U.S. Coast and Geodetic Survey marker at the top of the promontory in the background calls the hill Cooper Point. COLLECTION OF THE LATE GEORGE WILKIE.

Connecticut River Steamboat Company was incorporated, its two boats, the *Ellsworth* and *Macdonough*, could carry parties only as far as Greenwich.[11] But three years later the *Fulton* lost its monopoly, and thereafter, service between Hartford and New York boomed. A newspaper advertisement gave the schedule for the Connecticut River Steamboat Company's three boats. One of them sailed north every day and returned south the next day. There were sailings every day except Sunday. The fare from Middletown to New York was one dollar (meals extra).

Steamboats began stopping at Ely's Landing as early as 1822. To accommodate the traffic, large docks with warehouses were built alongside the ferry ramp. There are no piles today to indicate the location of the docks, but photos show them to have

In the foreground are the remnants of the steamboat dock at Ely's Ferry. The building to the south, a railroad freight house, still stands. COLLECTION OF THE LATE GEORGE WILKIE.

been substantial, dwarfing the ferry ramp and buildings. Sometime later, about 1840, additional docks of comparable size were built roughly one hundred feet farther south to handle freight. The freight building and its supporting dock have been rebuilt by the present owners.

The advent of steamboat traffic on the Connecticut River and the possibility that Ely's Landing would become a stop for the boats probably account for the change that occurred in the old Ely mansion in the early nineteenth century. A contributing factor, undoubtedly, was the fact that members of the Ely family no longer wanted to live there; possibly, increasingly busy ferry use disturbed them. Whatever the case, ownership of the house passed out of the Ely family temporarily in 1817. Many names appear on the deeds of sale. This suggests that the buyer was a syndicate that believed the house had business potential.

The Ely mansion became the Ely Tavern.

The only things that are left of it today are a cellar hole, foundation walls built of large stones without mortar, scattered foundation walls of outbuildings, crudely shaped bricks, broken window glass, and a few nicely laid stone steps on the riverbank. The site is on private property and may be visited only with the permission of the owners. But the cellar hole is only a few feet from Ely's Ferry Road and, without trespassing, you can see it as a sharp depression overgrown with briars, poison ivy, and brush.

What happened to the ancient building? No one really knows. The abandonment of the Pettipaug-Guilford Turnpike on the west side of the river in 1830 and the coming of railroads to Connecticut in 1839 undoubtedly reduced traffic at Ely's Landing and Ferry, so the tavern may no longer have been profitable. An 1854 map shows that the property was then owned by S.C. Ely, but the Ely family genealogy does not say that S.C. or any other Ely ever ran a tavern. If they did, they didn't run it for long because the genealogy says that the building burned down in about 1855. The Colonial Dames' *Old Inns of Connecticut*, on the other hand, reports the building was razed about 1875. There are two reasons to think that the Colonial Dames' statement is correct. First, an examination by the State of Connecticut's historic preservation officer found that no melted glass or charred wood is exposed in the cellar hole. Second, in his unpublished memoirs, Joshua Warren Stark used the later date (approximately) in the following story involving Samuel C. Ely. He wrote:

"Mr. Edward Brockway, who belonged to one of the best families in the town [Lyme] and lived in the house now occupied by Bertram Bruestle [on Joshuatown Road west of the Eight Mile River and just south of Old Hamburg Bridge], was very careful in all his dealings and noted for saving his pennies. It was about 1872, when the price of votes was the highest ever. Mr. Brockway, being

A schooner sailing north up the Connecticut River passes Ely's Ferry anchored in the foreground. This is the same as or exactly like the ferry shown in the 1879 oil painting by Carleton Wiggins (Page 126). COLLECTION OF THE LATE GEORGE WILKIE.

a Republican, approached one of the leaders of the Democratic party and after much bartering agreed that, if he voted at all, he would vote the Democratic ticket, for which promise he received $20. Then he approached the leaders of his own party and said 'I am sorry that I cannot vote for your candidate today, but I have made a promise that, if I vote at all, I will vote Democratic.' Of course, they didn't want this to happen, so they gave him $15 to not vote Democratic. So he received $35 and did not vote at all.

"The next morning he went to Essex by way of Ely's Ferry. Samuel C. Ely lived in the big house by the ferry. He was manager of the ferry, president of the Essex bank, one of the leaders of the Republican party, and his wife was a sister of Mr. Brockway. It so happened that he, on his way to the bank, crossed the river on the same boat that Mr. Brockway did. When he saw him, he said, 'Edward, I noticed you did not cast your ballot yesterday.' Edward replied, 'No, I didn't, Samuel; the truth of the matter is your town has become so corrupt that I wouldn't vote anyway.'"

Our knowledge of the Ely Tavern's operations during its short lifetime is as inadequate as our knowledge of its demise. The only thing known for a fact—this was probably a high point in the building's history—is that in 1833, during Andrew Jackson's presidency, he toured New England and stopped briefly at the tavern. His route took him from New Haven to Hartford. The steamboat *Waterwitch* then took him to Middletown and, after a reception there, carried him to Lyme where he was put ashore on June 18 at Ely's Landing en route to Norwich. The June 24, 1833 Hartford, Connecticut *Courier* reported: "At Lyme Ferry he went on shore and took a carriage which was provided to convey him to Norwich." The June 19 Norwich *Courier* said in part: "Yesterday a similar committee (the names of whom we are not enabled to give) went to Essex Ferry, and in conjunction with the former attended the President to the Turnpike Gate." Although neither paper mentioned the Ely Tavern, the president, who was very fatigued, must have used its facilities.

Although the Elys apparently had no direct connection with the Ely Tavern during its heyday, some of the tavern's secrets must lie with fifth- and sixth-generation Elys in the Ely Burying Ground on Tinker Lane about a hundred yards south of Ely's Ferry Road.

The Ely Burying Ground is one of numerous family cemeteries in Lyme and Old Lyme, and probably the largest and most beautiful. Surrounded by towering conifers, it lies open, bright,

The Ely Burying Ground, off Ely's Ferry Road. All descendants of Richard Ely I can be buried here. PRINT FROM THE ELY ANCESTRY, 1902.

and warm under the blue sky. Near the center of the large plot is the reddish-brown monument—suggestive of a sea captain's chest or a miniature oriental temple—of the first Richard Ely and his wife Elizabeth. Arranged around it—not pressing too close; in informal array—are the graves of his descendants and a tiny hand-ful of early-day paupers to whom the family felt it owed a final shelter.[12] About twenty of the old markers that had been broken by falling tree limbs or had simply crumbled away have been replaced with new. And here and there are the brand-new markers of the recent dead. Anyone descended from Richard Ely I can be buried here. And the full names of the great majority of the occupants feature the name Ely. Indeed most of them had the last name of Ely. But there are also Sterlings and Seldens and Noyeses and Colts. . . .the Elys were and are a vast tribe.

What a reunion they could have had at the old Ely Tavern, bustling off Cullick Ely's Ferry from Essex, coming down the gangplank from steamers towering over the ferry landing, stepping down from the stagecoaches arriving from Norwich, Providence, and Boston! You can see it all now.

Meanwhile, the weed-grown cellar hole by Ely's Ferry Road is not completely quiet. The river still murmurs with the tide and laps against the stones of the ferry ramp.

~

CHAMBERLAIN FERRY *moved into his hand-built house on Ely's Ferry Road, overlooking the mouth of the Connecticut River, in 1960. A boatman, he used to be a field editor for* Waterway Guide. *He is presently working with the state archaeologist in trying to unearth more information about the Ely Tavern.*

~ VIII ~

MORE PEOPLE

by EUGENIA L. WEST

For 124 years, three generations of Ely doctors—father, son, and grandson—cared for the people of Hamburg Cove, the whole town of Lyme, and much of Old Lyme.

The first doctor, Josiah Griffin Ely, was born in 1829. Through his ancestor, Richard Ely, the doctor was a member of one of Lyme's first families, going back to 1665. By the time of Josiah's birth, the day-to-day scramble for survival was over. Cattle grazed in cleared fields. Apple orchards produced great quantities of cider. Footpaths had become dirt roads.

For young Ely, getting from place to place meant "legging it" or "hoofing it" or rowing across the river. In spite of the distances, he probably managed to be at the two big attractions of the year: Governor's Day at the Niantic Encampment and the Norwich Fair.

Josiah Ely graduated from Yale Medical College, married a neighbor, Elizabeth Chadwick, and lived in the old Point House that still stands on the north side of Hamburg Cove where it joins the Connecticut River. Sylvia Harding, a well-known Cove resident, says: "The first Dr. Ely delivered my father in the borning room—usually a small, warm downstairs room handy for the sick.

His son brought me into the world. In those days, a country doctor was like a member of the family. We were ever blessed to be so close to a doctor."

When the first Dr. Ely died in 1886 at age fifty-seven, it was recorded in *The Connecticut Valley Advertiser* that 700 people attended his funeral. "Among the rich and poor alike he labored, giving to each all that he could give, answering every call, and many times, as upon the day before his death, going when scarcely able to stand."

His son, Josiah Griffin Ely, Jr. (he did not use the "Jr.") was born in 1857. At that time, life in the Cove area was centered around the First Congregational Church. Local ladies belonged to the still active Ladies Benevolent Society, once called the Two Mites Society. In the one-room schoolhouse, boys teased the girls and made life miserable for young teachers. If sent on an errand to one of the general stores in the neighborhood, young Josiah probably sat on a long counter when there was no more space around the stove and heard talk of local and national politics. He may have scowled or giggled at the tales told of the skirmishes between local men and boys and "those damn furriners" in Essex across the river.

To learn social skills, there was Elliott Bigelow's dancing and singing school held upstairs in his barn by the Old Hamburg Bridge. Young Ely later became a recognized authority on the local wildlife. He was also a fine shot and an outstanding pitcher on the town's baseball team. According to Sylvia Harding, men got together on Sunday afternoons to play ball or quoits (horseshoes) if they couldn't get up a team.

As the son of a leading citizen, Josiah G. Ely's education continued until he completed post-graduate courses at Bellevue Medical College. In 1893, he married Claude R. Stark of Grassy Hill Road. An article in *The Connecticut Valley Advertiser* described the event:

"The natural attractions of the bride were enhanced by a becoming costume of cream colored bengaline...there were costly gifts, aggregating more than 600 dollars...at the table sat Mrs.

The three Ely doctors. Josiah G. Ely, Jr.,
(top left), Josiah Griffin Ely (top right),
PHOTOS FROM THE COLLECTION OF ELIZEBETH
B. PLIMPTON. *Julian Ely (right).* PAINTING
BY BORIS KUBLANOV IN THE LYME TOWN HALL.

William H. Stark, a relative of the bride who was the only person present who witnessed the marriage of the bride's parents. The aged lady entered into the spirit of the occasion with a zest that proved the happiness she felt in being allowed to participate in the marriage ceremonies of the family of which she was a member. Two pleasant hours were passed in social converse and the enjoyment of delicious refreshments." [1]

Claude and Dr. Joe, as he was called, had four children. The outpouring of grief at the death of their daughter, Rosemary, in 1918 at age 14, was noted by the *Connecticut Valley Advertiser.*

"...the entire town was enveloped in a cloud of sorrow when word was received that Rosemary Ely . . . had died [of pneumonia following influenza] at Howard Seminary where she had recently entered as a student." [2]

At the turn of the century, the automobile age was looming. According to Josiah's youngest daughter, Helene Ely Willett, her father was the first man in town to give up his horse and buggy. "It changed his practice," she says. "People ran to the windows to see Dr. Ely coming in his car. I used to ride around with him and sleep while he made his calls."

In 1904, Dr. Ely's sister, Julia, married a neighbor, William Marvin, who was an outstanding man in the tight-knit community. Also a first family descendant, he inherited a house (still standing north of the Joshuatown Road intersection with Hamburg Road) that was built by Elisha Marvin around 1738.

Will Marvin was a dairy farmer who sold milk to the neighbors, and he also followed a family tradition of public service. According to an elderly resident, "He headed the town, ran the town, recorded the Town of Lyme."

At a time when terms of office were measured in decades, Marvin was Judge of Probate for forty-six years. He also served as Town Clerk from 1896 until his death in 1949. He was elected, he said, because he had a house big enough to hold the town safe, estimated to weigh four tons. If he happened to be out, his wife, Julia, could issue a license, and as cars replaced horses, the Marvins kept a kettle at the roadside watering trough to cool steaming engines.

In 1947, more than 500 people attended a testimonial gathering at the Lyme School. "I feel most undeserving," Judge Marvin said, "and as I sat listening to the most flattering remarks of the previous speakers, I was reminded of a small boy who was endeavoring to lead a calf across a highway bridge. The calf balked at the

William Marvin, far left, with friends shoeing an ox. COLLECTION OF ELIZEBETH B. PLIMPTON.

Julia Ely Marvin, left, with friend at the old watering trough in front of the Marvin house on Hamburg Road. COLLECTION OF ELIZEBETH B. PLIMPTON.

first plank and neither pulling, pushing, or beating had any effect. An auto approached and it was suggested that a blast of the horn might start the animal ahead. Placing his car immediately behind the stubborn calf, the obliging motorist sounded a loud toot, whereupon the frightened creature broke his rope with a bound, leaped the railing, plunged into the stream, and was swept away by the current. Turning to the driver, the boy exclaimed, 'Mister, that was too big a toot for so small a calf.' The lad's remark expresses my feelings at the moment." [3]

A neighbor and friend, Joshua Warren Stark, was less modest about his friend William Marvin: "No one knows, not even himself, how much time he has spent giving advice which has been earnestly sought, and in most cases, followed. No one knows but himself how many Domestic Relations' cases have been brought before him unofficially. No one knows but himself how many homes he has saved from destruction." At the dinner, Judge Marvin gave the guests a sample of his domestic philosophy:

"For a long time, I have had in mind a plan for making marriages more successful. You know the old saying, 'The straightest way to a man's heart is through his stomach' and 'To hold a man, feed the brute' . . . therefore, I suggest a law which would provide that a marriage license shall not be issued until after the bride-to-be has served the town clerk a satisfactory meal prepared entirely by her own hands. Of course, either the town or the state should provide some form of insurance for clerks, to cover sickness and death resulting from the tests." [3]

In 1935 when the second Dr. Ely died of pneumonia, the funeral was held in the Marvin home. At the time of his death, Ely was health officer, medical examiner, and a member of the board of education, posts he had held for many years. According to an obituary in the *New London Day*: "His cheering smile and personal charm won enduring friendship." [4] And in another testimonial: "...many have been the times when he has remained at the bedside of a delirious mother or child all night, forgetful of himself, and many times has he been called from his warm fireside at night to drive ten or fifteen miles to visit one of his sick patients…"

The third Ely doctor, Julian, lived to see great changes in Hamburg Cove. In 1894 when he was born, social life still revolved around the Cove. Neighbor still depended on neighbor. In 1887, the Public Hall Association began to organize community events. As always, dancing was a drawing card: an old Public Hall program lists seventeen dances, from Grand March to Quadrille, ending with the playing of "Home Sweet Home." The Grange, founded in 1896, became the sponsor of the Hamburg Fair. Older residents remember the fairground filled with oxen. A long walk for animals who came from Grassy Hill and Hadlyme, but for owners, it was a rare chance to buy, sell, make up a fine matched team—and try for a prize.[5]

Then in 1928, the dirt road from Old Lyme was covered with macadam as far as Grange Hall at the corner of Sterling City and Hamburg roads. Beyond, Old Hamburg Road was still known as the mud flats—cars had to be pulled out by ox teams—but the Reynolds' general store had a gas pump, the third in the state. Lord's Store put in a luncheonette and a soda fountain.

Dr. Julian Ely graduated from Harvard Medical School and was serving as a staff surgeon at Lawrence & Memorial Hospital in New London when his father died. He took over the practice, but broke with tradition by marrying a girl from Massachusetts. May Ely settled in and played the church organ for more than thirty years.

Like his father before him, Julian Ely held daily visiting hours in his own home. According to Rowland Ballek, as told to Lee Howard of the *New London Day*: "He would never say very much. Just a lot of 'yeps' and 'nopes'…. He had a little office with a card file. He'd have your whole life's information on a card." There was no secretary and no appointments—first come, first seen. Pills were given out in little white envelopes.

In the mornings, wearing a suit, tie, and hat and carrying an old black bag, Julian Ely made calls, first in a Studebaker, then a

Ford, charging $10 to $15 for a house call. Office visits were $5 to $10. It was his custom never to bill after the death of a patient—or there might be no bill at all. Payment in kind could be a game bird or side of venison. He was considered a good diagnostician. An old friend, on meeting him, said:

"Julian, I've got a pain."

"Where?"

"Here."

"Gallstones. Go have them out."

He didn't take back-talk from patients who were in trouble. Called to the bedside of a New Yorker who had recently moved to Lyme, he quickly discovered the man had an aneurysm and ordered him to proceed to the nearest hospital. The patient objected. "I'm going to Columbia-Presbyterian in New York."

"You can go there if you want," the doctor said. "But you're going to Lawrence and Memorial first. Right now!" The man did as he was told and sang Julian's praises ever after.

In the Ely tradition, Julian Ely had many interests. He loved to fish. He also played the violin. Sylvia Harding remembers get-togethers with the doctor and his fiddle, her mother at the piano, and the neighbors singing along.

In 1980, at age eighty-six, Julian Ely had a heart attack while seeing patients in his office. He died a few weeks later, a blow to the community. In emergencies, the first impulse had been to "Call Doc Ely." He was often the first to reach the scene of an accident. Said one ambulance volunteer: "He'd stay and help out any way he could." [6]

And, "if you got sick in the night, he would come," recalls Jane DeWolf. "It made you feel secure, that he was nearby...there's really no one to replace him. It's the end of an era."

An era of one hundred and twenty-four years of continuous care and service. A proud, possibly unique medical record set by the three Ely doctors of Hamburg Cove.

Julian Ely was six years old when, on May 1, 1900, a new family arrived in Hamburg Cove, one that would add to the older first families' imprint. As the boat from New York pulled into the landing, the Czikowskys were launched into life on the eighty-five hillside acres on Joshuatown Road that they had purchased for $700.

Eugene Czikowsky had been born in Prussia in 1865. He married Annie Zear, and they emigrated to Brooklyn, New York, where their first five children were born. When their daughter, little Minnie, was stricken by spinal meningitis, they were advised to move to a place with sweet water.

The first years on the Cove were rigorous. Sons William and George cleared the land for farming. Eugene, a butcher by trade, went out and bought an old fish cart. As told by William to Charlotte Ryerson of the *Gazette*: "He'd [Eugene] be on the road days, selling meat, butchering along the way . . . people bought a quarter of beef, and they'd hang it in the attic. When they wanted a chunk of beef, they'd saw out a piece, it stayed frozen all winter."

Two more children were born. The meat business expanded into farming, wood-cutting, a dairy—and the well-known general store. Enlarged in 1914, the store stocked dry goods, dairy products, a case full of candy, wheels of cheese, molasses in kegs, kerosene, grain—to list just a few items.

Rosemary Czikowsky Fox, Eugene's granddaughter, remembers when the store delivered daily orders:

"It catered to the needs of people who couldn't get out very much unless they had a horse . . . The family worked long hard hours. It was nothing to them to have a key and deliver an order, put it in the refrigerator, and go on to the next house. At two in the morning, they'd still be down at the barn milking. Then the milk had to be separated and bottled. They were well known for their raw milk and thick cream. Morning came early. Milking had to be done again, then gardening, haying, store tending." Older Cove residents remember when they heard cows being called in for milking in the middle of the night.

In the early days, according to Rosemary Fox, the uncles attended kitchen dances on Joshuatown Road. At home, there

Eugene and Annie Czikowsky came from Prussia by way of Brooklyn to Lyme in 1900 and settled on what is now called Czikowsky's Hill overlooking the Cove's Upper Bay.
COLLECTION OF ROSE-MARY CZIKOWSKY FOX.

were evenings of singing and always Gabriel Heatter and the news. For a long time "the store was never closed. Families would come in the evenings to buy food, ice cream for the kids, and beer to drink while sitting on the store porch."

Before automobiles, customers were often on sled runners from the middle of October to the first of April. Later, there were other problems. In her history of Brockway's ferry, Elizabeth Putnam describes Joshuatown Road as a very narrow dirt road.[7]

"The first hill was named Jared Daniels' Hill, then above Czikowsky's store, it became Jed Brockway's Hill.... Of course, the roads were not plowed, and the first car had to 'break out the road.' If you had trouble on Czikowsky's Hill, you could stop at the store, and Herbie and Gene Czikowsky would put a bag of grain in the trunk to add more weight in the back. The next day, you returned the grain."

Father Eugene lived to seventy-nine in spite of losing both legs. (The cause was blood poisoning brought on by diabetes and from dropping large pieces of meat and ice on his feet.) He insisted on watching the first amputation, saying, "It's my leg, I want to see you do it."

After the second leg went, however, the patriarch was forced into a wheelchair. When the family made butter on Sunday afternoons, as they always did, he was able to help by holding a small churn in his lap.

"He loved flowers," says Rosemary Fox. "Once when the hillside below the house was covered with violets, I picked him a big bouquet. He thanked me, and then he said: 'Flowers belong outside. Bring just one from now on.'"

Eugene died in 1944, and his wife Annie went a few months later. Minnie, who never married, ran the store and looked after the two bachelor brothers, Eugene and Herbert. She was known for her saving ways, always comparing prices in the Montgomery Ward and Sears Roebuck catalogs before ordering work clothes for the men. Rosemary Fox remembers that she and her brother used to pick strawberries for a small sum—and were told firmly

The Czikowsky store on Joshuatown Road—the source of everything, at all hours, from food to kerosene to animal fodder. COLLECTION OF ROSEMARY CZIKOWSKY FOX.

not to put the biggest berries on the top. To their annoyance, Aunt Minnie always put half of what she owed them into war bonds. Years later, this was much appreciated.

Before his death, Herbie Czikowsky gave up running the store, but he was still farming. One summer day in 1973, he went out on his tractor to mow. Watchful neighbors noticed that he didn't come home. He was found pinned under the tractor. It had overturned and killed him.

Herbie was the last second-generation member of this remarkable family, but other Czikowskys are still in the area. The land, roughly 320 acres, was placed in trust for six nieces and nephews. In the mid-1980s, the sale of part of this acreage sparked an epic local debate on the pros and cons of development. Steven Slosberg, reporting in the *New London Day*, wrote: "This [Hamburg Cove] is heaven, and if residents have to share it, damn few angels are going to get in."[8]

The Czikowsky store is gone today, but except for a couple of new houses on the steep hillside below and the many more boats in the water, the view from where it stood is hardly changed.

In the 1990s, Hamburg Cove and the surrounding country are almost the same as they were when William Lord and Richard Ely bought the land from the Mohegan and Nehantic Indians in the seventeenth century. Nature's plan for the area remains. Although numerous buildings have been introduced, most are hidden in the forest. The shoreline is essentially as it was. Cardinals and mockingbirds have joined the flocks of birds; otherwise, the wildlife is much as Chief Joshua knew it. The trees change as the older ones fall. Today the hemlocks, like the chestnuts before them, are slowly dying, but they will be replaced by other trees and shrubs. Hemlocks that have already been removed have opened up large stands of mountain laurel, whose growth was previously stunted by the conifers' sun-shield. In 1992 the laurel bloom was the best in a generation at least. Nature has a way of taking care of herself. With vigilant care, Hamburg Cove can continue to be a place of delight and peace.

~

EUGENIA L. WEST *is a novelist and is currently working on a series of mysteries. She has lived in one of Sterling City Road's old houses since 1978. Her father was chaplain of Yale University.*

The Red Barn *by Bruce Crane (1857-1937) looks south, across Joshuatown Road, to the Eight Mile River. Oil on canvas.* COLLECTION OF CHARLES CLARK.

∼ ENDNOTES ∼

II
A BLESSED PLACE

1. William F. Stihl and Evan Hill, *The Connecticut River*, 26.

2. Roger Duncan and John P. Ware, *A Cruising Guide to the New England Coast* (1972), 112.

3. *The Yachtsman's Bible, The Waterway Guide, Northern Edition*, 103.

4. John W. Hartman, *Pictorial Gazette*, Aug. 29, 1992. Originally published in the *Ocean Free Press*, Key Largo, Fla., April 1, 1992.

5. *Town of Lyme Annual Report*, 1990, 87.

6. Daniel P. Jones, *The Hartford Courant*, June 6, 1992.

7. Bruce P. Stark, *Lyme, Connecticut—From Founding to Independence*, 70.

III
THE SURROUNDING COUNTRY

1. Michael Bell, *The Face of Connecticut—People, Geology, and the Land* (Connecticut Geological and Natural History Survey, Hartford, Conn, 1985), 148.

2. Janet Radway Stone, geologist, U.S. Geological Survey, Hartford, Conn. Interview with John H. Noyes re the formation of Hamburg Cove, 1992.

3. William Cronon, *Changes in the Land—Indians, Colonists, and the Ecology of New England* (Hill and Wang, New York, 1983), 32.

4. Ibid, 28.

5. James E. Harding, *Lyme Yesterdays—How Our Forefathers Made a Living on the Connecticut Shore* (Pequot Press, Stonington, 1967), 42.

6. Ibid, 55.

7. Ronald Wesselon and George R. Stephens, *Hemlock: Its Insect Pests and Prognosis.* (Connecticut Woodlands, Connecticut Forest and Park Assn., Middlefield, Conn., Fall 1992), 8-9.

IV
THROUGH ARTISTS' EYES

The information for this chapter was primarily provided in interviews with Sylvia Harding, Elizebeth Plimpton, Leland Reynolds, and Roger Dennis. Jeff Cooley, Tony Whitley, Timothy Foley, Nelson White, Patricia Shippee, and Michael Lloyd aided with research.

Names and dates of noncontemporary painters mentioned are:

George Francis Bottum 1828-1879
Bertram Bruestle 1902-1968
George Bruestle 1872-1939
Harold Saxton Burr 1889-1973
Egbert Cadmus 1868-1939
William Chadwick 1879-1962
Winfield Scott Clime 1881-1958
Margaret Miller Cooper 1874-1967
Bruce Crane 1857-1937
Hugh de Haven 1895-1979
Charles Ebert 1873-1959
Oscar Fehrer 1872-1958
Eugene Higgins 1874-1958
Wilson Irvine 1869-1936
Albertus Eugene Jones 1882-1957
Charles R. Kinghan 1895-1984

James Goodwin McManus 1882-1958
Gertrude Nason 1890-1968
Thomas Nason 1888-1971
Edward Rook 1870-1960
Allen Butler Talcott 1867-1908
Will S. Taylor 1882-1968
Charles Vezin 1858-1942
Bessie Potter Vonnoh 1872-1954
Robert Vonnoh 1858-1933
Carleton Wiggins 1848-1932
Guy Carleton Wiggins 1883-1962

V
OF SHIPS AND SHAD

1. James Moran, *The (Old Saybrook) Gazette*, "Industry Boomed at Reed's Landing," Oct. 26, 1978.

2. Thomas A. Stevens, *Old Lyme: A Maritime History*, 1972.

3. Chamberlain Ferry, *Waterway Guide: Northern Edition*, "Connecticut River Cruise," 1984.

4. James E. Harding, *Lyme Yesterdays*, 1967. *Lyme As It Is and Was*, 1975.

5. Bill Thorndike, *The (Old Saybrook) Gazette*, "Reed's Landing Eyed as a Historical Site," Feb. 18, 1981.

6. May Hall James, *The Educational History of Old Lyme, Connecticut, 1635-1935*, 1939.

7. Barbara Deitrick, editor, *The Ancient Town of Lyme*, 1965.

8. Edmund Delaney, *The Connecticut River: New England's Historic Waterway*, 1983.

9. John V. Goff, *The Connecticut Historical Society Bulletin,* "Traces of the Shipyard Worker: Shipbuilding in the Connecticut River Valley, 1800-1850," Jan. 1981.

10. R. G. Albion and others, *New England and the Sea,* 1972.

11. Howard I. Chapelle, *American Small Sailing Craft, 1951; Boatbuilding,* 1941.

12. Charles F. Waterman, *Fishing in America,* 1975.

13. Douglas D. Moss, undated pamphlet of the Connecticut Board of Fisheries and Game, "A History of the Connecticut River and Its Fisheries."

14. Bruce Stark, *Lyme, Connecticut,* 1976.

15. Mel Allen, *Yankee,* "The Shad Always Come Back," May 1980.

16. Ogden Tanner, *Connecticut Magazine,* "Mad About Shad," May 1987.

17. *Bulletin of the Connecticut Historical Society,* "Connecticut River Fishing Piers," April 1949.

18. Elizebeth B. Plimpton, *As We Were on the Valley Shore,* "Valley Shore Fishing."

19. Brenda Milkofsky, *The Steamboat Log* of the Connecticut River Museum, "Springtime Means Shad Along the River," April 1986.

20. James Moran, *The (Old Saybrook) Gazette,* "Lyme Woman, Group Strive to Save Shad Fishing History," Nov. 9, 1978.

21. Maynard Bray, *Mystic Seaport Museum Watercraft,* 1979.

22. Elizabeth Putnam, *History of Brockway's Ferry - Lyme, Connecti cut,* 1991.

23. Tape recording of Allan Bartman, Roon Tooker and Norris Joseph at the Connecticut River Museum.

24. "Connecticut Waterman: Oliver LaPlace and River Valley Decoys," pamphlet for an exhibit at the Connecticut River Museum, 1983.

25. Edward R. Ricciuti, *Audubon Nature Yearbook,* 1987, "Shad: Poor Man's Salmon."

Also, conversations with Brenda Milkofsky, curator, and Robert Harvey, librarian, at the Connecticut River Museum, and with Fred Calabretta, oral historian at the Mystic Seaport Museum.

VI
STERLING CITY AND HAMBURG

1. Rogers, Lane, Selden, *Selden Ancestry,* 1931, 66, 68.

2. Research of Susan Hollingsworth Ely.

3. William Marvin, *Historical Address, First Congregational Church of Lyme,* Aug. 22, 1926, 13.

4. Mary S. Bakke, *A Sampler of Lifestyles,* (Advocate Press, Inc., New Haven, 1976), 97-99.

5. William Marvin, *Historical Address,* 11.

6. Albert M. Sterling, *The Sterling Genealogy* (Grafton Press, N.Y.), Vol 1: 338-41.

7. Unidentified newspaper clipping, "Reminiscences of Long Ago."

8. William Marvin, *Historical Address,* 14, 15.

9. *North Lyme Cemetery,* Secretary's Book.

10. William Marvin, unidentified newspaper clipping, "Fair Retains Old Fashioned Aspects."

11. Joshua Warren Stark, unpublished memoirs.

12. William Marvin, *Historical Address*, 16, 17.

13. Elizebeth B. Plimpton, *Lyme Public Hall, Chronology;* Joshua Warren Stark, unpublished *Memoirs; New London Day; Sound Breeze,* April 1880; Andrew Spitzler, *The Gazette,* "Fire House to be sold to Association," Dec. 12, 1985.

14. *Charter of the 8-Mile River Channel Company,* papers of James L. Lord II.

15. Joshua Warren Stark, unpublished memoirs.

VII
THE ELYS AND ELY TAVERN

1. *The Ely Ancestry,* Calumet Press, 1902.

2. May Hall James, *The Educational History of Old Lyme, Connecticut, 1635-1935,* 248.

3. Statement of George Wilkie, October 1967.

4. *Records of the State of Connecticut 1800-1801,* Vol. X, 105.

5. *New London Day,* Sept. 20, 1977.

6. Records of the Essex Historical Society.

7. Statement of George Wilkie, October 1967.

8. Statement of M. H. Francisco.

9. May Hall James, *The Educational History of Old Lyme, Connecticut, 1635-1935,* 131.

10. Edmund Delaney, *The Connecticut River* (Globe Pequot Press, 1983), 106.

11. May Hall James, *Educational History,* 121.

12. Statement of John H. Noyes.

VIII
MORE PEOPLE

1. *Connecticut Valley Advertiser,* June 3, 1893.

2. Ibid, Oct. 11, 1918.

3. William Marvin, speech at Lyme School, Nov. 15, 1947.

4. *New London Day,* Jan. 27, 1935.

5. Joshua Warren Stark, unpublished memoirs.

6. Lee Howard, *New London Day.*

7. Elizabeth Putnam, *History of Brockway's Ferry - Lyme, Connecticut,* 1991.

8. Steven Slosberg, *New London Day,* Dec. 11, 1985.

∾ INDEX ∾

Italicized page numbers denote illustrations